MW00415819

This book, while presented as a "how-to" guide for firearms, should never be used as the sole resource when purchasing, using or selling firearms. This book is intended to give the reader an idea of how firearms work and what the laws regarding their purchase, use and disposal are in the United States and is by no means a definitive resource. Readers should become familiar with the local laws and seek expert advice before engaging in any activities involving firearms. The author is not responsible for any illegal activities or accidents of any kind resulting from a misinterpretation of this publication.

Getting Started with Firearms (Rev 1.1)

About the Author

Nick Leghorn is a graduate of Penn State University currently working in San Antonio, Texas. He was born in New York City and grew up in the area, the son of a rather strict "anti-gun" family. He shot his first gun in the Boy Scouts and was instantly hooked on shooting sports.

While attending Penn State, Nick started practicing Olympic smallbore rifle with the Penn State Rifle team. After only a few months of practice he was performing well enough to begin competing against other schools with the team. During his senior year he started branching out into different types of competitions, including USPSA handgun shooting (production division), NRA/CMP High Power Rifle (Service Rifle division), and eventually 3-gun (Tactical Optics division). He also founded and runs his own competition shooting team, consisting of dozens of members in multiple states and countries, who all compete and share tips and information together.

Nick is a writer for The Truth About Guns, the most popular firearms blog in the United States, where he publishes regular articles about firearms, ammunition and related equipment. His main areas of interest in shooting are competition sports, long range accuracy, and scientific testing. He really enjoys using his knowledge of statistics and analytical abilities to solve questions and do interesting experiments with firearms.

In his free time (what's left after writing for TTAG, at least) he's a volunteer firefighter and EMT with a local fire station and enjoys lockpicking.

Table of Contents

Foreword

There are two ways someone gets involved with firearms. Well, three ways, but we're only counting the legal version of the word "involved" today. Either you're introduced to firearms as a kid and it's a family tradition, or you're introduced later in life by some kind person who shows you the joys you've been missing. I was in the latter camp, being the son of a strictly anti-gun mother and growing up in the suburbs of New York City. Guns were considered a "problem" that needed to be "dealt with," and anyone who strayed from the party line was looked down upon.

That all changed in college when I started practicing with the Penn State rifle team. I was bitten by the bug of competition shooting, but I had a problem: I had no idea where to start.

I've written this book as if I was going to hand it to myself that first day after rifle practice, when I started down this journey. I wanted to create something that was tangible and could be passed to newer shooters to give them the basic knowledge required to get out and start shooting safely and accurately from day one. It is my hope that this book helps the next generation of shooters to get up to speed safely and quickly so that they can share the fun and excitement of firearms ownership for years to come.

Firearms Safety Basics

Before we go any farther we need to talk about firearms safety. Statistically speaking more people are injured by playing golf than are injured at the shooting range, but the only way to keep that number low is by adhering strictly to the four major firearms safety rules.

The "four rules" were originally penned by Jeff Cooper, one of the foremost experts in small arms in the 20th century. The rules have changed little over the years, and a good shooter will have them memorized and follow them religiously every time he or she is on the range. These are the rules that keep us safe, and any breech is cause for immediate concern. So learn them by heart before stepping onto the range.

The four basic firearms safety rules are:

1. **Treat every gun as if it were loaded.**

The vast majority of accidental injuries and deaths from firearms happened because someone thought the gun was unloaded and did something stupid, including one case where a young man put his "unloaded" pistol up to his head and pulled the trigger – an action that caused his death.

If you always treat every gun as if it were loaded then the one time you accidentally forget there's a round in the chamber no major harm will come. And trust me; it will happen eventually that you forget. Go look up the number of instances where police officers have accidentally fired their guns while cleaning them, it's astonishing.

2. **Never point the gun at anything you do not intend to shoot.**

The firearms rules are all about minimizing the possibility of an accidental shooting. Rule #1 was about mindset, written in the hope that a person who believes a gun may be loaded will use their God given common sense and not do anything stupid. Rule #2 is a more specific rule, one which follows logically from Rule #1:

If your gun is never pointed in an unsafe direction then even if it were loaded and accidentally discharged nothing bad would happen. A little bit of extra awareness on your part (called "muzzle discipline" in firearms parlance) makes it much less likely to lose something you don't want to part with. Like your TV. Or an appendage. Or your child. Or your life.

3. **Keep your finger off the trigger and outside the trigger guard until you have made the decision to fire.**

In order for the gun to fire, a number of actions need to happen in sequence. First you need to have a gun, then it needs to be loaded, then it needs to be ready to fire with the safety off, then you need to put your finger on the trigger, and finally the trigger must be pulled. Any break in this sequence will result in a gun that doesn't fire. Rule #3 is designed to be that break in the chain of events that prevents an accidental shooting even if all of the other safety rules have been broken.

If you keep your finger outside the trigger guard then it's much harder to accidentally jerk your finger and fire the gun.

4. **Be aware of your target's foreground and background.**

When aiming a gun it's very easy to focus all of your attention on the target and forget about what's in front and what's behind. Bullets don't just magically appear on a target and then immediately stop; they fly from your gun and don't stop moving until they hit something solid. Even if your target is a bad guy or a deer the bullet can still be deadly after it passes through their bodies and comes out the other side.

8

When doing any kind of shooting it is imperative that you make sure to know exactly what is between your gun and the target, and whether there's anything hiding behind your target. For example, if you're shooting from behind a concrete wall sometimes your sights will be visible and seem to show a clear path to the target but your barrel will still be blocked by the wall. If you shoot in this situation there's a good chance that you can be injured by flying concrete when the bullet strikes the wall.

You and you alone are ultimately responsible for your own safety no matter where you are, which means not only following the rules yourself but watching to make sure that everyone else is following them too. If you see something unsafe say something, whether by calling a "cease fire" (more on range commands later) or simply talking to the person concerned.

If at any time you feel it is unsafe to remain at a firing range, **LEAVE**! Your life and your health are not worth risking just because it's inconvenient to drive all the way to the range and then having to leave without being able to shoot.

Why would anyone want a gun?

Firearm ownership is on the rise. More people than ever before are buying and shooting guns in the United States, and there are a number of reasons for that. We'll quickly cover some of the more popular reasons, but there are always more.

Recreational Target Shooting

There's something magical about making a projectile hit a target. Humans have been trying to hit distant targets since the beginning of time when the first caveman chucked a stone at a tree. Targets can be anything from nicely printed bull's-eye posters to tin cans on a rail fence, but the joy of having a shot land exactly where you aimed it is universal. I can't begin to count the number of times I've taken an anti-gun person to the range and let them shoot at some steel targets for the first time, only to have them pester me forever after to go again.

Target shooting is a great way to relax. The process of setting up the gun, putting the sights on target, controlling your breathing and getting the perfect trigger pull has been found to be very similar to meditation and has many of the same calming effects, especially with smaller caliber firearms. And when using reactive targets (like cans or steel plates) there's an instant reward for a well-placed shot that becomes addicting.

Competition Target Shooting

Ever since that first caveman chucked a stone at a target, some jackass has been there to claim he can to do it better. And so competition shooting was born.

Competition target shooting is about being able to put a round through a target more accurately than the other guys. In some competitions they also time how long it takes and put up obstacles for the shooter to move through. No matter what you want to do or shoot there's probably a competition organization set up to do exactly that, from Cowboy Action (where competitors dress in 1890's clothing and shoot at Old West themed targets) to F-Class (where shooters place precisely aimed shots at a target up to 1,000 yards away).

The most popular competition shooting sport is called 3-Gun - basically you use a rifle, a pistol and a shotgun (hence 3-gun) to physically move through stages and shoot at a variety of targets, all while being timed. The fun thing about 3-Gun is that the majority of the targets are reactive, including steel plates and clay pigeons, so the adrenaline of being under the clock mixes with the "reward" for well-placed shots, making it the favorite sport of adrenaline junkies.

Long Range Precision Shooting

There are a special breed of people who believe that a shooting range should begin at 1,000 yards (~3/5 of a mile). These people typically use large caliber firearms to fire projectiles from one hilltop to another at extreme distances, using steel plates as targets so they don't have to drive a mile away to check paper targets for holes. This kind of shooting requires not only good firearms handling skills but also a keen knowledge of physics and mathematics and an understanding of how air currents and even the movement and curvature of the earth affect the flight path of a bullet. The appeal is not only bragging rights to the furthest shot but also the joy of putting theoretical physics to practical tests.

Hunting

When I started writing this book I had never been hunting. Halfway through the first draft one of my friends who lives in Texas invited me down to his ranch to give it a try, and I must admit that it's addictive.

Hunting combines the biggest challenges of competition shooting (specifically accuracy under pressure and firing from a less than ideal shooting position) with the added challenge of finding your prey. Animals have evolved over the centuries to evade predators (like humans) and they do a very good job of not being seen, so finding them and getting a good shot at an animal takes some serious skill. Even after you've found an animal and have set up for the shot you have the further problem of a target that could move at any second, and once you fire your gun the animal will immediately run away. It creates an extremely stressful situation that requires practice and concentration to be successful, which is my idea of a fun time.

In my experience, hunting isn't really about killing animals. Hunting is about spending weeks at the range honing your skills and perfecting your equipment with an actual goal in mind (rather than simply punching holes in paper for no reason at all), spending quality time with friends, and enjoying nature. While I was out hunting I let more animals walk right by my shooting position than I ever tried to shoot and I enjoyed that as much if not more than taking the shots that bagged me my two bucks. The meat in my freezer that is the result of that hunt is just the delicious icing on the cake.

There are also a large number of people in the United States that survive primarily on animals they have harvested themselves through hunting. Wild animals provide an excellent source of protein and are much less expensive than store bought meat, and eating locally grown food reduces pollution and is much greener for the environment.

Collecting & History

There's no denying that firearms have changed the world. Just in the last 250 years firearms helped created the United States, caused the loss of an entire generation in World War I, and stopped an evil dictator or two during World War II. During that time frame firearms have undergone a more rapid advance than in the previous 300 years since their invention, producing ingenious solutions and mechanisms designed to make them easier to fire, more accurate and faster. Some people (like me) find beauty in mechanical ingenuity and want to have functioning versions for their own collection. For these people firearms are like works of art, to be admired and cherished.

Also, just like art, firearms can be expensive. Rare models or unique pieces can bring hundreds of thousands of dollars. Civilian legal machine guns (more about legality later) have arguably been a better investment than even gold recently. For this reason some collectors not only enjoy the aesthetics of their collection but use it as a way to invest their money without playing the stock market or other traditional methods.

Self Defense

This last reason is the one that is gaining the most popularity. As budgets are being examined and police response time is widening from a few minutes to over an hour, citizens are taking their protection into their own hands. The ability to protect one's home and family from an intruder is something that is so popular that I'm being asked for recommendations of firearms for that purpose at my day job.

There are a number of different shades of "self defense" situations for which people buy firearms, and often they are concerned about multiple possible scenarios. Some scenarios people want to protect themselves against include home invasions, rape, violent assaults and the zombie apocalypse or other similar societal collapses. While each of these scenarios has a relatively small probability of taking place the fact is that they have happened (with the exception of the zombie apocalypse... so far) and will happen again, and some people have made the decision to spend money on protection in the event that they do happen.

Buying self defense firearms is like buying insurance, except if used properly they keep bad things from getting worse instead of trying to clean up the aftermath.

How a gun works / Parts of a gun

In order to safely and effectively use a firearm you need to understand how it works, both on a mechanical and ballistic level. Sure you could probably do OK with a "point this end at the target and pull that trigger" approach, but that's not what you're going to get from me. People who I take shooting get a nice half hour lesson on the finer points of how a gun works, but depending on how fast you read it might not take you that long. So grab a snack, it's time for school.

How a Gun Works

Firearms have evolved a lot over the last few hundred years. Modern firearms are both more complicated and more reliable than the earlier versions, but that does mean that there are more parts to be familiar with. The basic idea behind a firearm hasn't changed in centuries and it's pretty simple:

The basic concept behind how a gun works, ANY gun, is pretty simple. A projectile is placed in a tube or "barrel", and then some force is applied to accelerate it out the other end. The projectile then flies through the air until it hits a target. Just like when you shot spitballs at your classmates in school, this concept works very well in the small scale for things like tiny pieces of wet paper and even small darts in blowguns. But when the projectiles are larger and the targets further away, more force is required.

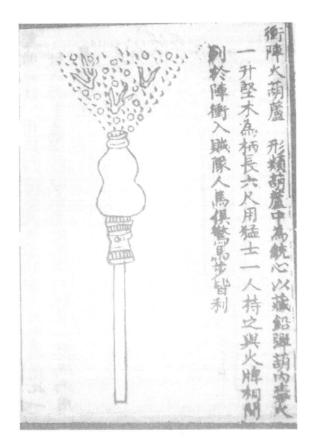

衝陣火葫蘆 形類葫蘆中為銃心 以藏鉛彈葫內盛火藥半斤

一升堅木為柄長六尺用猛士一人持之與火牌相間

則於陣衝入賊隊人馬俱驚寫笰皆利

Luckily, a compound was discovered ages ago in China that would provide that force. Gunpowder is a granular substance that burns (not explodes) very quickly, creating a lot of expanding gases. When used in a gun, the powder is loaded at the bottom of the barrel and then a projectile is placed firmly on top sealing in the powder. Once the powder is ignited these gases become trapped in the barrel behind the bullet and start looking for a way out; the only way for them to escape is by pushing the bullet out of the way. These gases push the projectile out of the tube faster than any man can blow, even heavy projectiles made of lead. The earliest firearms, of which the musket is a prime example, required the powder and projectile to be loaded separately each time the gun was to

15

be fired and ignited the powder using a sparking "flintlock" mechanism or a very hot piece of slowly burning rope called a "slow match."

Muskets are known as "muzzle loaders" because that's how you load them; from the front opening or "muzzle" of the gun. The musket is a long metal tube into which you pour some gunpowder and then shove a projectile. It's simple and it works, but because the powder and projectile are loaded separately it takes a while to load and is sensitive to changes in the weather. Starting in the 1800's a new way of loading a firearm was devised, one which used a self contained package that sped up the process of loading and firing the gun.

Modern firearms use a self-contained "cartridge" that neatly packages the gunpowder, the projectile, and a mechanism to ignite that gunpowder all in one easy-to-use object that can be loaded quickly into a gun. Instead of the spark or flaming rope, all that modern firearms do to ignite the gunpowder is tap on a "primer" at the back of the cartridge that is sensitive to sudden increases in pressure and responds with a small spark. The primer then catches fire and ignites the rest of the powder. From there the concept of operations is the exact same as it's always been: A projectile being forced out of a tube by expanding gasses. Guns that use self-contained cartridges are usually referred to simply as "modern firearms."

Parts of a Gun

Depending on what specific type and model of firearm you have some of the parts may be different. However, there are a set of common parts that every modern firearm has.

- **Barrel** – This is the long metal tube down which the projectile is pushed.
- **Chamber** – At the end of the barrel closest to you is the chamber, or more technically correct "combustion chamber," where the gunpowder is initially ignited. It's a sealable end of the barrel that has been hardened to handle the intense pressure created by the expanding gasses. In modern firearms this is where the cartridge is placed.
- **Breech** – The breech is the term for the end of the barrel closest to the shooter. The breech seals the barrel and makes up the rear of the chamber. The breech is typically the most heavily hardened part of the gun because it is subjected to the highest pressures.

- **Muzzle** – The far end of the barrel is where the projectile eventually exits the gun and begins its flight to the target. This open end of the gun is called the "muzzle" of the gun.
- **Trigger** – Guns usually have a small metal tab protruding beneath the gun called a "trigger." This metal tab is connected to the mechanisms inside the gun that sets off the primer and ignites the powder, expelling the projectile down the barrel of the gun. It "triggers" the mechanism, and so is logically called a trigger. The trigger is located immediately in front of the rearmost grip protruding beneath the stock.
- **Trigger Guard** – In order to keep things from accidentally grabbing onto the trigger and setting off the gun (especially when walking around in the woods where branches may snag passing travelers) guns are fitted with a metal loop around the trigger called a "trigger guard." As the name implies it guards the trigger against accidentally being pulled.
- **Receiver** – The piece of metal that houses all of the major components of the gun and holds them together is called the receiver. This scrap of metal is legally considered to be the firearm and will always come with a serial number.
- **Magazine** – Some firearms use a magazine to hold cartridges ready for firing. Magazines use a spring or other mechanical device to automatically position a new cartridge for insertion into the chamber. Magazines can either be detachable or permanently affixed. These are sometimes confused with "clips" which perform a slightly different function. But more about that later.
- **Sights** – The sights on a gun are usually small metal pieces attached to the top of the gun that help the shooter aim the gun and hit the target. We'll get more into sights in a second.

Numerous firearm designs have been created over the years to solve one simple problem: How do you get the cartridge into the chamber efficiently? The mechanism that places the cartridge into the chamber and seals it off is called the **action** of the firearm. There are many different types of actions, but the following are the most common seen in firearms.

The action is considered **closed** when the bolt is forward and locked against the barrel, forming a seal and leaving only one end of the barrel open. An action is **open** when the bolt has been drawn back away from the chamber and the barrel is no longer sealed on one end, allowing air and light to pass through the barrel from one end to the other.

- **Muzzle Loader** – These firearms technically don't have an action. With a muzzle loading firearm the powder and projectile are loaded separately, and by hand, from the muzzle of the gun and packed against the breech inside the barrel. Once the gun is fired the shooter repeats the process, loading the gun manually each time.
- **Break Action** – With a break action firearm the barrel snaps in half to reveal the chamber and allow the shooter to place cartridges in the gun. Usually the breech and the chamber are housed in separate sections of the firearm and positioned on a hinge to allow them to be separated for reloading and sealed for firing.
- **Bolt Action** – Bolt action firearms use a metal rod that moves back and forth called a "bolt" to extract spent cartridges, load fresh cartridges, and seal the chamber of the gun. Bolt action firearms require the user to move the bolt directly by hand.
- **Lever Action** – Lever action firearms work on the same principle as the bolt action but use a lever underneath the gun to move the bolt back and forth. The advantage is that less force is required to move the bolt and the firearm can be operated much faster.
- **Pump Action** – Pump action firearms are similar to lever and bolt action firearms but use a grip positioned in front of the chamber that moves back and forth to operate the bolt. These are most commonly found on shotguns.

- **Blowback Operated Action** – This is the simplest semi-automatic action. The force of the expanding gasses push the cartridge out of the chamber and move the bolt backwards as well, ejecting the spent cartridge. Once the cartridge is extracted a magazine positions a new round for insertion and a spring forces the bolt forward against the chamber once again.
- **Recoil Operated Action** – This is the most common semi-automatic action. The force of the bullet flying down the barrel causes the barrel itself to move backwards rapidly. That rapid rearward movement is translated to a bolt which uses momentum to continue backwards after the barrel has stopped, extracting the spent cartridge. Once the cartridge is extracted a magazine positions a new round for insertion and a spring forces the bolt forward against the chamber once again.
- **Gas Operated Action** – These are the most reliable semi-automatic actions. A small hoe is drilled part way down the barrel through which some of the expanding gasses are channeled. These gases push against the bolt and cause it to move backwards extracting the spent cartridge. Once the cartridge is extracted a magazine positions a new round for insertion and a spring forces the bolt forward against the chamber once again.

Ammunition

Ammunition is the word used to describe a collection of cartridges for use in firearms, just like a herd of cattle or a murder of crows. The singular word for ammunition is a "cartridge" or "round," as in "hand me that round of ammunition." As I explained earlier, a "cartridge" is a self-contained unit that holds the bullet, gunpowder and some sort of pressure-sensitive primer together to make it easy to load into the firearm. The cartridge is held together by the "case" or "shell," which is extracted after the gun is fired.

Centerfire vs. Rimfire Ammunition

There are a couple different "types" of self-contained ammunition (holding the bullet, the powder and a primer in a self-contained cartridge) that have developed over the years, but the two most prominent types are "rimfire" and "centerfire" ammunition. Each cartridge type contains the same components (primer, powder, bullet and case) but the configuration of those parts is what differentiates them.

- **Centerfire ammunition** uses a self-contained, pressure sensitive primer placed in the center (hence the name) of the back of the cartridge. This primer can be replaced and the ammunition "reloaded" in order to keep the cost of shooting down.
- **Rimfire ammunition** uses a primer that can be activated by striking anywhere along the outside rim located at the rear of the cartridge. This is much more convenient for smaller calibers as a standard centerfire primer would not fit in the case, but the cases cannot be "reloaded." Rimfire cartridges typically cost only a fraction of the amount that centerfire cartridges cost.

What does "Caliber" mean?

Technically speaking, the "caliber" of a firearm is a measurement of the diameter of its barrel (and how big a bullet you can cram down it). However, thanks to the advent of "modern" ammunition the definition of caliber has changed slightly.

These days the "caliber" of a firearm describes the size of the bullet and the length of the cartridge that works in a specific gun. Ammunition (and firearms) is available in a staggering number of different "calibers," and more calibers are being added every day.

It is EXTREMELY IMPORTANT that shooters only use ammunition with the same caliber specifically indicated for their gun. Failure to do so could lead to the gun exploding and your death. Sorry to be a Debbie Downer, but I had to say it.

Caliber is usually indicated either in the metric (European) or Imperial (American) designation. While these designations provide some basic information about the ammunition (and to keep confusion at bay no two calibers share the same designation) there's much more information required in order to actually manufacture the rounds. Caliber information is only designed to ensure that shooters use the correct ammunition in the correct guns.

Metric caliber designations follow the [bullet diameter]x[case length]mm[extras] formula for naming, and use the diameter of the bullet in millimeters as the leading number. For example...

- **7.62x51mm NATO** ammunition means the bullet is 7.62 millimeters in diameter, the case is 51 millimeters long, and the ammunition specification was designed by NATO (the North Atlantic Treaty Organization).
- **7.62x54mmR** ammunition means the bullet is 7.62 millimeters in diameter and the case is 54 millimeters long. The "R" designation means that there is a rim around the edge of the case.

23

- **5.45x39mm** ammunition means the bullet is 5.45 millimeters in diameter and the case is 39 millimeters long.

I think you get the idea. While 7.62x51mm NATO and 7.62x54mmR use the same diameter bullet the fact that their cases are different lengths means that they are not interchangeable. And while the NATO ammunition will fit in a 7.62x54mmR chamber, firing it would be exceedingly dangerous if not deadly.

Imperial designations are... strange. The vast majority use a [bullet diameter] [developer name] format and record the bullet diameter in terms of inches, but some substitute other text at the end. For example...

- **.308 Winchester** is the Imperial designation for 7.62x51mm NATO ammunition because the bullet is .308 inches in diameter and Winchester is the name of the company that patented the cartridge in the United States.
- **.30-06** is the name for a popular hunting round in the United States that uses a bullet with a .3 inch diameter and was developed in 1906.
- **.30-30 Winchester** is a popular caliber for lever action hunting firearms that uses a bullet with a .3 inch diameter and is loaded using 30 grains of gunpowder. The cartridge was developed by Winchester and so that company's name is at the end.
- **.22 LR** is a popular rimfire cartridge that uses a bullet with a diameter of .22 inches. The "LR" stands for "Long Rifle," which differentiates it from the "Short" version of the round which contains less powder and is shorter.
- **.700 WTF** is the name of a cartridge recently designed for long range shooting which uses a .7 inch diameter bullet. The round is so big that the typical first remark people make is "what the f#$& is that?!" and so he added "WTF" to the end of the designation.

Even though .308 Winchester and .30-30 Winchester use the same diameter bullet and are designed by the same company, the fact that their names aren't EXACTLY identical means that they're unsafe to be used interchangeably and doing so could be very harmful to your health.

Caliber information for firearms is available on the barrel of the firearm and the side of the box of ammunition. Again, PLEASE make sure you match the barrel caliber to the ammunition caliber EXACTLY or else bad things could happen.

Shotgun Ammunition

Shotguns are the special snowflakes of ammunition. Instead of firing cartridges, shotguns fire "shells," and used shells are called "hulls." Even more confusing is that because shotguns are designed to fire multiple small pellets (called "shot") instead of only firing one single solid piece of lead (like rifles) there are three numbers used to describe the ammunition: One number describes the diameter of the shell, another describes its length, and a third describes its contents.

Gauge (Diameter)

Shotgun shells, like wire, are measured in "gauge." As in "I have this 12 gauge shotgun." The way you measure gauge is by first determining the largest sphere of solid lead that will fit down the barrel of your shotgun, then calculating how many of those spheres it would take to weigh 1 pound. Or you could cheat and look at the barrel of your shotgun where the manufacturer has conveniently placed that information.

All you really need to know is that the "standard" shotgun is a 12 gauge shotgun. If the gauge is higher than 12 (20, 28, etc) then the shotgun has a smaller diameter barrel (because more lead spheres would be required to equal one pound of lead). If the gauge is lower (10, 4, etc) then you're going to have a very sore shoulder.

Length

The second number on a box of shotgun ammunition or your barrel will tell you the length of shell you can safely use. This will typically either be 2 ¾ or 3 inches, but you should pay close attention not to use 3 inch shells in a 2 ¾ inch gun. Even though the difference in length is very small, using a larger shell than recommended may cause the gun to explode. Yes, explode.

Shot Size and Type

We're past the measurements where your shotgun can blow up so take a deep breath. "Shot size" is a measure of the size of the little pellets in your shell. Just like with the gauge, smaller numbers mean bigger pellets. But there's a twist – there are three "types" of shot. Yeah, they don't make it easy.

- **Birdshot** – This stuff is designed for hunting birds and shooting clay pigeons at the shotgun range, and so the pellets are very small and a whole bunch are crammed in each shell. #7 shot is the "standard" size, with #8 shot being slightly smaller and #6 shot being slightly larger.
- **Buckshot** – These pellets were designed to bring down warm blooded mammals, and are used both in hunting and home defense. As such they are quite a bit larger, and pack a bit of a punch. #00 Buckshot is the standard size, and you get less than 10 pellets per shell.
- **Slugs** – OK, not technically "shot," but it's still a type of projectile that can be fired from a shotgun. Slugs are solid pieces of lead (like a bullet) that are fired through a shotgun. They don't have the same accuracy and distance that a rifle round has, but they're more accurate than birdshot or buckshot and have been known to stop a deer in their tracks.

Types of Firearms

There are a number of different types of firearms, including rifles, shotguns, and handguns. There are many other different types of firearms, but new shooters really need only concern themselves with the three described below.

Rifle

Just about everyone knows what a rifle is and looks like, but in terms of legality there are a few requirements that a firearm has to meet in order to be considered a rifle. A typical rifle meets these criteria:

- Designed to be fired using two hands and braced against the shoulder.
- Fires a single solid projectile with each pull of the trigger.
- Uses a system of spiral grooves to "spin" the projectile (called rifling).
- Fires a bullet with a diameter no larger than ½ inch.
- Has a barrel length of more than 16 inches

Rifles are usually used for shooting at long distance targets, and often come with telescopic scopes. Examples of rifles are the Remington 700, AR-15 / M-16 / M4 and AK-47. The AR-15 is currently the most popular firearm design in America, and is used for everything from hunting to target shooting.

Shotgun

A shotgun is distinctly different from rifles or pistols because instead of using a grooved barrel to stabilize a single bullet a shotgun uses a smooth barrel and fires a chunk of tiny little pellets. The idea is that throwing dozens of pellets at a target gives the shooter a better chance at getting a hit. This works great for targets like flying objects so long as they're easily breakable or relatively small. Legally speaking, a shotgun meets these criteria:

- Designed to be fired using two hands and braced against the shoulder.
- Fires a single round of ammunition with each pull of the trigger.
- Uses a smooth barrel.
- Has a barrel length of more than 18 inches.

Handgun / Pistol

The terms "handgun" and "pistol" are used almost interchangeably to describe the same thing. Legally, a handgun is a firearm designed to be fired with one hand and no support from the shoulder, and has a barrel length of less than 16 inches.

Describing Firearms

Firearms are described using information about their action, type and caliber. For example:

- **"Bolt Action Rifle in .308 Winchester:"** A rifle (fired from the shoulder, 16+ inches barrel length) that operates using a bolt action and uses ammunition marked ".308 Winchester."
- **"Semi-Auto Handgun in 9mm:"** A handgun that automatically loads a new round of ammunition whenever it is fired and fires a bullet that is 9mm in diameter.

Anything more than that is icing on the cake. If you're looking in the classified ads for a gun you might also see the type of sight used on the firearm. Which brings us to the next section...

Types of Sights

It's very hard to hit a target if you have no idea where the gun is aimed. Sights help the shooter align the barrel of the gun properly so that the projectile will hit the target.

Sights come in two varieties, either a mechanical form or an optical form. Mechanical sights use pieces of metal fixed to the top of the gun and receiver to identify where the gun is pointing, using two different pieces of metal that must be properly aligned. Optical sights have only one piece and typically project a crosshair or dot on top of the target to identify where the gun is aimed. Optical sights are considered to be easier to use but are much more expensive and not as common.

Mechanical Sights

There are a number of popular designs for mechanical sights, but they all use a 2-piece system. The "rear sight" is the closest to the shooter's eye, and the "front sight" is the furthest away (typically on or over the muzzle of the gun). In order to hit a target these two pieces must be properly aligned over the target. Here are some popular sight designs and how they should be aligned.

	Patridge	Aperture	Diopter and Globe
Front Sight			
Rear Sight			
Properly Aligned			

Typically iron sights are aligned such that the top of the front sight is centered in the rear sight. With sights like the Patridge sight, the top of the front sight (called a "post") should be level with the tops of the rear sight as well. The target would be placed either on the tip of the front sight post or in the middle of the front sight (if using a diopter and globe).

Optical Sights

While mechanical sights need to be aligned in order to function properly, optical sights don't need that same treatment. Optical sights come in two flavors, telescopic sights (that magnify the image and make small targets appear larger) and 1x optics (that do not magnify the target). The benefit to optical sights is that they are faster and easier to use than mechanical sights, but on some guns (and in some types of competitions) they either don't make sense to use or are not allowed. Optical sights can and have been placed on every type of firearm.

Telescopic sights are typically seen on long distance precision rifles where the target is 50 yards away or farther. The magnification assists the shooter in seeing the target and makes it easier to line up a shot. Telescopic sights typically have a crosshair (which looks like the + sign) or other similar marking inside the scope that provides a point the shooter can use to place on the target to aim the gun. Telescopic sights have mechanisms built in that allow the location of that aiming point to be changed to line it up with where the barrel is pointing. The process of making the barrel and the sight line up is called "zeroing" the rifle, and we'll discuss that more later.

1x optics do not magnify the target, which is ideal for "close quarters" fighting or situations where the target is closer than 50 yards. These optics are generally either a "red dot" design that projects a virtual dot on an image of the target or a "holographic" design that does the same thing using lasers. As with the telescopic sights these have adjustments built in such that they can be zeroed as well.

Firearms and the Law

Before I get into this, I just want to say that I am not a lawyer. This section DOES NOT constitute legal advice, and you should check current Federal, state and local laws before purchasing a gun. The best method is to actually go and talk to a reputable firearms dealer, who will be happy to instruct you on the best method of legally handing them money in exchange for a gun.

Whenever I talk about shooting to someone who has never done it question #1 is "is that legal?" And yes, yes it is. In the United States, at least. For the most part.

In the United States there's no recreational activity more closely regulated than the shooting sports, and for those of us who are law abiding citizens want to enjoy our chosen hobby it's an unfortunate fact of life, but the basics of how gun laws in the United States work can be easily explained. There are three basic types of firearm and each one has specific legal definitions that I'll quickly explain, as well as some restrictions on ownership. But first some general restrictions and definitions.

Semi-Automatic versus Fully Automatic

Firearms can be broken into three broad categories based on how their triggers work. Two categories can be purchased cheaply and without many restrictions, and the other costs multiple thousands of dollars and involves extensive background checks and fingerprinting.

- **Manual** firearms require the shooter to physically load each round of ammunition into the gun. These are generally slow to fire, and include lever action, bolt action, and pump action firearms.
- **Semi-Automatic** firearms fire a single round of ammunition when the trigger is pressed, then automatically cycle the action and load a new round of ammunition but do not fire again unless the trigger is released and pressed once more. One trigger press = one round.
- **Fully automatic** firearms will continuously fire round after round of ammunition once the trigger is pressed until there is no more ammunition available to the gun (either in the magazine or other

feeding mechanisms). One trigger press = multiple rounds. These are commonly known as "machine guns."

The "General Restrictions" below apply to manual and semi-automatic firearms but not fully automatic firearms. Fully automatic firearms (or "machine guns") can be purchased, but there are some gigantic restrictions and massive waiting periods involved. We'll get to that later.

General Restrictions

In order to buy or possess a firearm in the United States you need to meet a set of criteria set forth by the Gun Control Act of 1968. Specifically, you cannot own or possess a firearm if you are:

- Convicted or accused of a crime for which the sentence is 1 year in prison.
- A fugitive from justice.
- An unlawful user of or addicted to a controlled substance (such as marijuana or cocaine).
- Adjudicated as mentally defective or committed to a mental institution.
- An illegal alien.
- Dishonorably discharged from the military.
- Someone who has renounced your U.S. Citizenship.
- Subject to a restraining order.

To make sure that only people who meet those criteria are allowed to purchase firearms the U.S. Government (and specifically the Bureau of Alcohol, Tobacco, Firearms and Explosives or BATFE, also referred to as the "Bureau of Fun Things") set up and regulates a system that grants pieces of paper called "Federal Firearms Licenses" or FFL. The way the system works is that only people with an FFL can ship and receive firearms through the mail, which means if a citizen wants to buy a new gun the only way to do it is through a federally licensed dealer.

In order to purchase a firearm from a FFL, Federal law requires you to also be:

- 18 years or older for a shotgun or rifle
- 21 years or older for a handgun

Individual states place further restrictions on who can purchase what types of firearms and how many can be purchased in a given time period. For more information about that check the "Common Gun Control Measures" section.

When you go to purchase a gun from an FFL you will be asked to fill out something called a "Form 4473." That's the ATF designation for the piece of paper you sign certifying that you're not a felon or dishonorably discharged or anything else that would keep you from buying a gun. Once you complete the 4473, the FFL will perform a background check on you using a system called the National Instant Check System or NICS that will verify most of the information. In addition, state laws may also require the FFL to use local databases as well as NICS. Lying on a form 4473 is a crime, and law enforcement officers will often be dispatched to arrest those caught trying to buy a firearm while disqualified from doing so.

There are other ways of buying guns, specifically "private party" transfers, but that's not something I recommend for a new firearms owner until they have a good understanding of the local laws. If you want to know how private party transfers work, look for a firearms website or forum specific to your state (like PAFOA for Pennsylvania, Virginia Gun Trader for Virginia, MD Shooters for Maryland, etc.) and start reading.

This gets complicated if you live in places that are less than friendly to firearms, like New Jersey, California, Illinois, Washington, D.C., New York State or New York City. These locations place additional restrictions on the purchase and possession of firearms so make sure you check local laws before buying one.

For the rest of the country, once your background check is complete you can walk straight out of the gun store and enjoy your new purchase. There are some catches and caveats, but those are specific to individual types of firearms.

Common Gun Control Measures

Federal laws haven't changed all that much since 1986 when the Firearm Owners Protection Act kicked in, but state and local laws change all the time. I wanted to include a gigantic table giving some basics on laws in each state, but after discussing that idea with the readers at my blog I decided instead to outline some of the typical "gun control" laws your area may have enacted in an attempt to keep guns out of the hands of dangerous criminals and what that means for law-abiding citizens. This should give you an idea of what's out there without accidentally providing out of date or incorrect information.

Firearms Permit

Some places, specifically Illinois, Massachusetts and New York City, require citizens to apply for and obtain a permit of some sort simply to possess a firearm in that jurisdiction. While the permit process would appear to allow any law abiding citizen to obtain a firearm, they are often subject to approval by local law enforcement who can deny any application for any reason.

Firearms permits can be required for ownership of all firearms, ownership of certain types of firearms (usually handguns), or only for the purchase of those firearms. Permits to purchase a firearm typically have a short window of time (a few days) for the citizen to complete the transaction before the permit expires and the citizen must go through the process again.

Permits typically require the prospective firearms owner to fill out an application and questionnaire, submit to a background check, and may also require character references and interviews with local officials before the permit is granted. In other words the process is a gigantic pain in the ass.

Firearm Registration

Some areas require that firearms be registered with the local law enforcement agency. Usually only certain types of firearms need to be registered (those deemed likely to be used in a crime), and more often than not those firearms are handguns.

Registration of a firearm usually includes the make, model and serial number of a firearm, but some jurisdictions also require a "ballistic fingerprint" of the firearm as well. The ballistic fingerprint includes a spent cartridge from the firearm in question as well as a bullet which has been fired through the gun and recovered. The firearm leaves telltale marks on these pieces and it is believed that by having a searchable record of the components they can be matched to those found at a crime scene and traced to the owner.

Registration can take place before the firearm is purchased (usually via a permit to purchase), at the time the transaction is completed, or in some cases within a given time frame after the transfer is complete. Registrations usually need to be kept up to date, and it's the duty of the firearm owner to ensure that the records are accurate.

Storage Requirements

Safe firearm storage is essential for firearms ownership, but some areas mandate how a firearm can be stored. For example, Washington, D.C. requires handguns to be stored unloaded and either completely disassembled or with a "trigger lock" that keeps the gun from being fired until it is unlocked with a key. Handguns must also be locked in a storage device separate from any ammunition. The observant reader will note that this makes it extremely difficult to load a firearm in a hurry in home defense situations, a point currently being argued in the legal system.

Assault Weapons Ban

The Federal Government enacted a 10 year "assault weapons ban" or AWB in 1994 that forbade the production or sale of certain types of firearms to civilians. The law was designed to restrict or eliminate the ownership of firearms with a certain appearance rather than a specifically dangerous function and so its criteria are based on those physical characteristics. While the federal AWB expired in 2004 and those firearms were once again legal on a Federal level, certain states enacted their own copies of the AWB that are still in place today.

The term "assault weapon" comes from the German MP-44 Rifle, or as Adolf Hitler liked to call it his "*sturmgewehr*". The literal translation of the term differs between "assault rifle" and "storm rifle" depending on who you ask, but since "assault rifle" has a more negative connotation and evokes a scarier image that's the one that stuck.

The AWB bans the sale or manufacture of semi-automatic rifles capable of accepting a detachable magazine and having two or more of the following features:

- Folding or telescoping stock
- Pistol grip
- Bayonet mount
- Flash suppressor or a threaded barrel designed to accommodate one
- Grenade launcher (or a muzzle device designed to launch grenades)

Also banned were the sale of "assault pistols," which were semi-automatic pistols capable of accepting detachable magazines and having two or more of the following features:

- Magazine that attached outside the pistol grip
- Threaded barrel to accept barrel extensions, flash suppressors, handgrip or silencers
- Barrel shroud with a hand hold
- Unloaded weight of 50 oz. or more
- A semi automatic version of an automatic firearm

Finally, semi-automatic shotguns with two or more of the following features were also banned:

- Folding or telescoping stock
- Pistol grip
- Fixed capacity of more than 5 rounds
- Detachable magazines

The Federal AWB included a "grandfather clause" that allowed firearms legally possessed before the ban went into effect to be exempt from the new laws, and that grandfather clause was adopted by the states that implemented their own version as well. So, if you bought your rifle in 1993, the new laws didn't apply to you. However, starting in January of 2013 some states have tried to remove that clause from the books. There's some debate about whether that action constitutes an "*ex post facto*" law (one which makes an action that was legal when performed illegal after the fact, and is unconstitutional) and/or violates the 4th amendment protection against unreasonable search and seizure of property.

Magazine Capacity Restrictions

Some areas place restrictions on the size of magazines available to civilians. That means a gun cannot have more than a certain number of cartridges loaded at any time. These restrictions typically apply to "detachable" magazines and not internal magazines, although some areas restrict that as well. The idea is to slow down "spree killers" by forcing them to reload more often, although there have never been any conclusive studies proving this theory.

<u>Waiting Period</u>

A waiting period is one of the most common forms of gun control and can take many shapes. The common reason for implementation is to keep people from becoming enraged and immediately purchasing a firearm to kill in the heat of the moment.

The most general form of waiting period on firearms starts from the moment the buyer concludes the sale of a firearm from a dealer and prohibits the buyer from taking ownership until a certain period of time has passed. For example, in Florida people who purchase a handgun must wait 3 days before taking ownership.

Other forms of waiting periods include a prohibition on the purchase of more than one firearm (or type of firearm) in a given period of time. For example, in Virginia citizens cannot purchase more than one handgun in a 30 day time period.

These laws often have exceptions built in for those with concealed carry permits (which prove they are responsible and have passed a background check) or law enforcement officers.

National Firearms Act Weapons

In 1934 the U.S. Congress enacted the National Firearms Act in order to regulate weapons that were being used by criminals, mobsters and bank robbers to terrorize the citizens of the United States. They didn't outlaw those weapons entirely, they simply made it so that anyone wanting to purchase one needed to pass a background check and pay a $200 tax (a substantial amount in those days). Some states outlaw "NFA Weapons" as these items are known, so check your local laws. I'm listing them all here because even though it's a pain to go through the process average citizens can still own these items.

While NFA weapons do mean that the owner has added responsibility to keep the government up to date with their home address, it does not grant the ATF the ability to search their house anytime they want (as some misinformed gun store owners might tell you). If you own one of these weapons the only "big" added headache is that the ATF has the right to request to inspect your NFA items (and ONLY your NFA items), and you can schedule that appointment whenever and wherever you want (within reason). It doesn't happen very often, and with the increasing number of NFA owners I'd expect it to be downright rare these days.

The following are defined as weapons regulated under the National firearms Act:

Machine Gun

A machine gun is a fully automatic firearm that fires multiple cartridges with a single press of the trigger.

According to the National Firearms Act every machine gun must be registered with the BATFE and only registered machine guns can be transferred to new owners. In 1986 the BATFE stopped accepting new applications to register machine guns for civilians. This enacted a de facto ban on new machine guns from being sold to U.S. citizens (except military and law enforcement) and consequently only machine guns registered before 1986 are legal for citizens to own. This has drastically increased the price of those machine guns and created a market where machine guns are purchased solely as investments.

Short Barreled Rifle

A short barreled rifle (or SBR) is a rifle with a barrel length of less than 16 inches or an overall length of less than 26 inches. These are sometimes referred to as "sawn off rifles" because they were often made by taking a hacksaw and cutting a normal rifle down to length.

Short Barreled Shotgun

A short barreled shotgun (or SBS) is a shotgun with a barrel length of less than 18 inches or an overall length of less than 26 inches. Like SBRs, SBSes are often referred to as "sawn off" shotguns.

Destructive Device

Destructive Devices (or "DD" as they're referred to) come in one of two categories.

- Explosives covered under the "DD" label are incendiary, explosive, grenade, rocket or poison gas emitting device with a charge of more than 4 ounces, a missile with a charge of more than ¼ ounce, or a mine.

- The other category of Destructive Devices are weapons that fire a projectile with a diameter greater than ½ inch. This includes most varieties of cannon and mortar, but there are some exceptions that are specifically allowed due to their "sporting" use.

Silencer

A silencer or suppressor is a device which makes the sound a gun makes when it goes off quieter. No device can ever completely silence a gun, but according to the original patent filing that was the name Hiram Maxim gave his invention and it has stuck ever since. Silencers are a booming industry (in size, not sound) and thousands of new silencers are sold in the United States each year.

I had a chance to ask the folks at Advanced Armament Co. (currently one of the largest civilian silencer manufacturers) why people buy a silencer, and the typical answer seems to be to protect their hearing. Firearms make a loud noise when they fire and silencers allow shooters to enjoy their time on the range without needing additional hearing protection, which is often bulky and uncomfortable.

With inflation driving down the perceived cost of the $200 tax stamp enough people have started buying silencers that the average wait time for paperwork to be returned by the ATF has more than doubled in the last year.

Any Other Weapon

As the name implies, the term "Any Other Weapon" or AOW is a catch-all category for firearms that the ATF determines need to be regulated. The best examples of an AOW are "disguised" firearms such as a James Bond style cane gun. AOW firearms are subject to a $5 tax instead of the full $200 tax but are still subject to the same paperwork and background checks.

Fundamentals of Shooting

It may seem like shooting is complicated, but in reality there are three things that a shooter needs to focus on while taking their shot: sight alignment / sight picture, trigger control and follow through.

Eye Dominance

First things first: You need to figure out which eye is "dominant."

Humans have stereoscopic vision, meaning they use two eyes that focus on a single point and the brain uses both images to form a composite that we "see" which gives us our depth perception. Just as some people are right or left handed, one eye typically is the dominant eye and is used to compose the majority of the image we see, while the other eye simply fills in the rest of the picture. The dominant eye is the one preferred for shooting because the image it produces is typically of slightly better quality and will focus on the sights faster and easier.

The test for eye dominance is simple, and can be done anywhere.

1. Pick a point on a far wall or a faraway object and focus on it.
2. Bring up your hands and place them flat, palm side out, on either side of the object in your field of view.
3. Using your thumb and index finger of either hand form a diamond with the object in the center of the diamond. Keep the object in focus the entire time and don't lose sight of it. The diamond should be only an inch or two across.
4. Bring the diamond back towards your face, not losing sight of the object the entire time. Bring your hands back until they hit your face.

At the end of the exercise whatever eye you can still see out of is your dominant eye. Often your eye dominance will correspond to your hand dominance, but there are a good number of people who are "cross dominant." Cross dominant people are, for example, left handed but right eye dominant. There are competing theories about whether it is better for cross dominant people to shoot with their dominant hand or not, but I've found that despite the initial discomfort, cross dominant people eventually shoot best using their non-dominant hand to pull the trigger. It takes practice, but the benefit is faster target acquisition down the line.

Sight Alignment / Sight Picture

The most important part of shooting a gun is aiming the gun. If your aim isn't exactly on target then no matter what else you do your bullet will not hit it. Thankfully there are some features on your gun (specifically the sights) that make this step a little easier.

The sights on a gun give the shooter an idea of where the bullet is going to impact and whether it will hit the target. We briefly discussed how sights worked, but now we'll go into a little detail on exactly how to use them.

<u>Sight Alignment</u>

This step is much more important for mechanical sights than for optical sights. With mechanical sights you have two different pieces that you need to align properly in order to determine exactly where the gun is aiming. If the alignment is even a little off the bullet may hit inches, or even feet, from your intended target.

Most mechanical sights use a "post" front sight (refer back to the section on sights for more information on posts). Patridge sights, for example, should be aligned such that the front post is level with the two nubs on the rear sight and equal amounts of daylight can be seen on either side. Aperture sights, which use a metal circle for the rear sight (like those on an AR-15), should be positioned such that the tip of the front sight is centered in the rear metal ring. When properly aligned the tip of the post will indicate exactly where the gun is aimed.

Some mechanical sights use a series of rings instead of a front post. These are typically found in competition rifles and precision firearms. When using these sights the rings should be centered within each other and the target (which is usually circular) should be centered within the front sight.

The reason for having all of the sights be properly aligned when centered is that the human eye is very good at telling when something isn't even or in the middle, and mechanical sights exploit that ability.

Even with optical sights some sight alignment is in order. Your sight should be placed between you and your target, level to the ground and directly in front of your face.

Sight Picture

Sight alignment is about getting the gun properly positioned so that the intended reference point for aiming your gun lines up with the actual place your barrel is pointing. Sight picture is about putting that aiming point on your intended target.

While keeping the proper sight alignment, the shooter should ensure that the reference point for aiming their firearm - whether the front sight post of a mechanical sight or the crosshairs of an optical sight - are lined up with where they want the projectile to hit the target.

Sight alignment and sight picture is the toughest part of aiming a gun, not because it's hard to get right quickly but because it needs to be maintained through the next step. And that could take a few seconds.

Trigger Control

The impulse new shooters have is to jerk the trigger. The gun is going to make a loud noise and move around and they want to get it over with. This approach inevitably leads to poor shot placement (not hitting the target). The reason is that the sudden movement of the finger on the trigger moves the firearm enough to screw up the shot, and also promotes "flinching" by the shooter (preemptively moving the gun to compensate for recoil). Flinching invariably causes the rounds to be way off target.

The solution to flinching and jerking the trigger is to squeeze the trigger instead.

The proper trigger pull involves the shooter slowly applying pressure until the gun goes off. This not only keeps the gun from being jerked off target by the trigger pull itself but also makes it so that it's a surprise when the gun goes off and this stops any flinching.

Follow Through

Even after the gun goes off the shooter has one last thing to do before they can start to prepare for another shot.

After firing new shooters have a tendency to immediately want to take their finger off the trigger and lower the gun to check their target. Unfortunately this eagerness to check your work has a tendency to throw off shots as well. There's a split second difference between when the trigger "breaks" and when the bullet leaves the barrel, and that eagerness can mean that the shooter doesn't maintain a proper sight picture through the entire process and subsequently can lead to missing the target. In order to keep the gun on target the shooter should "follow through" with the shot.

After the gun goes off hold the trigger back for a second or two. Take a short breath, and then release the trigger and lower the gun. This should ensure that the gun is on target as it is going off. Keeping the trigger held back after the gun goes off is called "follow through."

To review, the trick to hitting your target every time is following these steps:

1. Make sure your sights are properly aligned and you are aiming at your target.
2. Slowly squeeze the trigger - the gun going off should be a surprise.
3. Follow through with the shot by keeping the trigger pulled all the way back until after the gun has finished firing.

That's all there is to it. There are no secrets or tricks of the trade, just keep the three steps in mind and you'll hit the target.

Inspecting a Firearm / What to Do when you Pick Up a Gun

When I'm looking at a gun, whether I'm considering purchasing it, about to fire it, or just "trying it out," there's a process that I like to run through that covers all the major points that would detract from a firearm's accuracy or usability (and therefore its price as well).

Keep in mind that while you are doing these inspections you should be following the four rules, specifically the one about not pointing a gun at anything you don't intend to destroy. Pointing a gun at your buddy is the sure way to never be invited back to play with their guns.

Here's my process:

1. ENSURE THAT THE FIREARM IS UNLOADED

The MOST important step in firearms handling is ensuring that there is no ammunition anywhere in the gun. Firearms accidents can only happen when ammunition is in a gun, so by removing the ammunition we lower the probability of an accident. I personally enjoy being alive with all of my limbs intact and prefer to remain that way so I thoroughly check the firearm by performing three quick inspections with the gun pointed in a very safe direction:

- Remove the magazine from the firearm or, if the magazine is permanently attached, visually inspect the magazine and ensure that it is unloaded.
- Open the action of the firearm and visually inspect the chamber, ensuring that there is no ammunition in the chamber or the action.

- Work the action two or three times to ensure nothing comes out and no ammunition is left in the gun.

Every. Single. Time. Even if the gun is being handed to you by a gun store clerk who just performed the same inspection and certified it as being unloaded you NEED to check again. The one time you forget to do it is the one time you're going to accidentally shoot yourself.

2. Inspect the exterior of the firearm

Take a good long look at the outside of the gun. You're looking for:

- Gouges in the finish or the metal (bad for value, possible structural issues).
- Any bend in the barrel that is not symmetrical (possible safety issues).
- Any cracks in the stock or grips (evidence of poor maintenance, bad for value and safety).
- Any cracks in the action or the receiver (evidence of stress and structural issues, unsafe to fire).

These small clues should give you enough information about the general condition of the gun that you can fire it with relative confidence that it won't blow up. If there's even the slightest indication of issues (or you just want to be cautious) your local gunsmith will be happy to check it out for you and make sure it's safe.

3. Work the action of the firearm

On a rifle this means opening and closing the bolt, on a handgun this means moving the slide back and forth or cocking the hammer on a revolver, and on a shotgun this usually means pumping it a couple times. You're looking to determine how smooth the action of the firearm is, which will give an indication of the quality of the gun.

4. Pretend to fire the gun (dry fire)

After you check the gun one more time to make sure it's really unloaded, hold the gun as if you were going to fire it and pull the trigger. Make sure to properly align the sights when you're doing this. And PLEASE be sure to aim the thing at a wall or something solid, not people.

Pretending to fire the gun, or "dry firing" (the technical term), tells you everything you need to know about the gun without actually going to the range. How heavy is it? How does it feel? Is it comfortable? How does the trigger feel? Is it easy to pull? The only thing missing is the recoil of the gun going off.

The trigger and how it feels is of specific importance when you're dry firing a gun. I won't go into specifics right now, but there's an article in the appendix for this book that discusses triggers and how they should "feel" in much more detail. Give it a read when you get a chance.

5. Inspect the barrel

The last step I perform when inspecting a firearm is to check the barrel of the gun. This usually involves violating one of the four golden rules of safe gun handling as I have to point the gun at my eye to look down the barrel but it's a necessary step in the inspection process.

First you want to open the action of the firearm and make it stay open, usually by using the "slide stop" on a handgun or "bolt catch" on a rifle. Then you want to shine a dim light down the barrel through the open action. Now, when you look down the barrel from the front (muzzle) of the gun you should see the spiral pattern that make up the grooves in the rifling (or not, for shotguns). The barrel should be bright and shiny, free from any "rough" spots, and the rifling should seem to be clearly cut into the barrel (if present). It should go without saying, but there shouldn't be any "obstructions" in the barrel (such as rocks or other debris) as that could cause the barrel to explode when firing it.

Selecting your First Firearm

Buying a firearm is just like buying a car, and comes with many of the same hazards – chiefly the risk of being ripped off by used car (gun) salesmen. There are literally thousands of models of firearms in various flavors, colors and configurations on the market to choose from, and at the end of the day the "best" first firearm is the one that suits your own specific needs.

Before you ever set foot in a gun store, there are a few steps which you should take to help you decide on your first firearm.

1. **Determine your needs.**

The MOST important part of selecting a firearm is determining what you need the firearm to do. A few chapters ago we talked about why people want guns, and depending on which category applies to you your selection will differ. Some common categories of criteria for selecting a firearm are:

- **Accuracy**: Do you need to hit a target at extreme distances (1,000+ yards) with a precision placed round, or is a human sized target at 50 yards your idea of "long range accuracy?"
- **Speed**: Will one round do the trick, or will you need to fire additional shots quickly?
- **Size**: Does the gun need to fit in your trunk or in your pocket?
- **Target**: Will you be punching holes in paper, or do you need to take down a living target?

Also you should consider your body type and composition. Shooting is something that can be enjoyed by everyone, including people with disabilities, and that is because firearms can be molded to address any physical issue. For example, a Marine recently contacted me who had lost one hand and most of the use of the other hand while serving in Afghanistan. He wanted to continue shooting so he was looking for advice on how to configure his rifle to do so. With some simple modifications he was comfortably shooting once more. Any physical difference from the "normal" human, be it a missing appendage or simply being left eye dominant, can be accommodated as long as you realize your needs and look for a firearm that suits you.

2. Choose between a rifle, a handgun or a shotgun.

Once you understand your needs you can figure out what firearm works best to suit those needs. I'm just going to run down the categories I outlined earlier as the reasons people shoot and talk about what I think makes the best firearm for each situation.

- **Recreational Target Shooting**: Recreational target shooting is all about putting holes in paper targets at "short" distances (100-150 yards tops) and hitting other small targets. As a teen in the country my father used to line up tin cans on a railing and shoot them off, repeating the process all afternoon. For this kind of shooting a semi-automatic rifle in .22lr caliber will be ideal, probably a Ruger 10/22. It's easy to maintain, reliable, accurate, and the .22lr ammunition is dirt cheap and available everywhere. You might also want to consider a handgun in .22lr, but those are generally more expensive and subject to more restrictions.
- **Competition Target Shooting**: The specific firearm you purchase will depend greatly on the type of competition you want to do, as different competition types will require different guns. But if you're just looking for a good rifle to start practicing your accuracy then a bolt action rifle in .22lr, which means increased accuracy over the Ruger 10/22 while still keeping the price of ammunition low, is perfect for you.
- **Long Range Precision Shooting**: Long range precision is all about big bullets and bolt action rifles, like the Remington 700 or the

Weatherby bolt action rifles. Something in .308 Winchester would probably be ideal for people beginning this kind of shooting.

- **Deer Hunting**: In order to bring down a large animal it helps to use a large bullet. The most popular firearms are bolt action rifles in .30-06.
- **Bird Hunting**: Bird hunting is typically about trying to hit a moving target. Your best chance with moving targets is to use a shotgun, which fires a spray of deadly projectiles and makes it much easier to hit moving objects. 12 gauge pump action shotguns are my favorite.
- **Collecting & History**: There's really only one "first" gun for this category, and that's the Mosin Nagant model 1891/30 chambered in 7.62x54mmR. This rifle was the main firearm for the Russian troops in World War One and Soviet troops in World War Two and was mass produced in such astonishing numbers that a good Mosin Nagant rifle can be had for as little as $80. Every rifle has some history behind it, and they're cheap enough so that if you screw something up you can easily replace it.
- **Self Defense**: This is the only category where I would recommend a handgun over a rifle or shotgun. Handguns (pistols) have the benefit of being small and concealable while still packing enough punch to stop an attacker in their tracks. Check your local laws, but often the ability to carry a loaded handgun concealed on your person is only a permit application away and provides peace of mind when on the town.

Other guns may fit the bill for your specific needs, but these are my recommendations. Some people are automatically drawn to a specific firearm because it looks cool or they like something about it, and as long as you know how to use it I'm not going to argue against buying it. There's no point in buying a gun you don't like, and a gun you want to shoot will make you practice more and become proficient faster.

3. **Head to your local gun store and handle some guns.**

Now that you've figured out the outline of what you want, it's time to visit your local gun store — but not to buy. Let me emphasize that again: DON'T BUY ANYTHING YET. That's not the point of this trip; it's something to look forward to in the future.

The point of this particular trip to the gun store is to handle some of the firearms that meet your criteria and get an idea for how they feel in your hand. This is something that you're possibly going to be spending a lot of time holding, so it should be comfortable and natural to hold it and fire it. Gun stores also typically have a wide selection of firearms of a similar nature, so if you're looking for a handgun (for example) they will have a wide variety of models that you can try out and determine which ones you like best.

Another reason for this initial gun store trip is to tap into the font of knowledge that is the gun store clerk. Most gun stores are staffed by people who know what they're talking about and are happy to help you find what you really need (instead of what will get them the most cash), but every once in a while I do run into that "scumbag" gun store owner who will try to pressure you into spending too much and buying the wrong gun just to make a buck. That's why we're not buying anything this trip: to keep the gun store clerks from pressuring you into buying something you don't really want.

Remember the steps for inspecting a firearm and apply them to every gun you pick up, but be sure to ask the sales clerk if it's OK. Some clerks don't appreciate people picking up guns without permission, and others are OK with everything except dry firing the gun. It depends on the store, the clerk, and the gun in question so always be sure to ask.

Don't be intimidated by the gun store because you don't know the etiquette. There's an entire section in this book devoted to that question a little further along that you can refer to before setting foot inside a store.

4. Research & Choose a Caliber

Once you have an idea about what kind of gun you want the next step is to hit the internet and start searching for reviews and similar firearms. Is this firearm reliable? Does it have mechanical issues? What do other owners think of it? How about the guys at The Truth About Guns, what do they think? How expensive is this gun compared to similar firearms? All of these things should be investigated before deciding to buy a firearm.

While you're researching your firearm of choice you should also be considering which caliber of ammunition you're going to choose. The same model of firearm is often produced for multiple calibers, and caliber choice is typically secondary to model choice for this reason. For a "first" firearm I highly suggest something in .22lr, 5.56x45mm NATO, .308 Winchester, 9mm or 12 gauge 2 ¾ inch. These calibers of ammunition are commonly available at sporting goods stores and other retailers and are very inexpensive compared to some of the more "exotic" calibers, while still being deadly enough for use in a self-defense situation (yes, even .22lr).

5. Buy the gun

Once you've settled on a firearm and a caliber it's time to return to the gun store, but this time you don't need to leave your wallet in the car. Just stroll straight up to the counter and tell the clerk what you want, and if they don't have it in stock I guarantee they will happily order it for you. Make sure the price isn't too far over the advertised price on the internet.

Gun stores will be well versed in the local laws, so if you need any special permits or identification documents they will let you know and help you through the process of obtaining any necessary permits. They have a financial interest in seeing you become a lawful and regular customer, so they will be more than happy to help you understand the local laws and figure out any necessary paperwork.

6. Clean and Practice

Once you've actually made the purchase it's time to start learning how the gun works, how to clean it, and how to shoot it accurately. The first two can be done in the comfort of your own home (and should be done periodically), and the third should be practiced on the local firing range regularly. Especially if you intend to use this firearm for self-defense you should be well practiced in its use and accurate with it as well.

Firearms Etiquette – At the Gun Store and At the Range

There are two places that are unavoidable for firearms owners: The gun store and the firing range. At first they may seem to be intimidating places with strange and unwritten rules, but once you know the "lay of the land" you'll be able to blend right in.

At the Gun Store

The gun store is just like any other shop, except the clerks are armed and the merchandise requires a background check before you can take it home. There are, however, some things you should keep in mind when at the gun store.

First and foremost, your safety is paramount. All guns on display at a gun store SHOULD be unloaded, but if you see anyone flagrantly breaking one of the four "golden rules" I talked about at the beginning of this book you should probably make for the door and try a different store. Your life is too important to trust to minimum wage employees so be sure you keep an eye out for yourself. Trust me, there are likely to be better gun stores within driving distance – you just have to find them.

The cardinal rule for gun stores is to be polite to everyone you see, clerks and customers alike, and they will, in turn, be polite to you. If you're polite and they're being a dick that's a good sign that you should take your business elsewhere, as they're especially likely to try and rip you off with higher prices. On the other hand, if you're being a dick (pointing guns in people's faces, annoying the clerks or being rude in general) prepare to be asked to leave. Gun stores have the right to refuse service to anyone they want for whatever reason they choose.

Gun store clerks, like any other salesperson, are there to sell you their product. And like any other salesperson they can be hit or miss in terms of knowledge and attitude. The good gun store clerks will be able to talk to you about the differences in the various firearms and help you identify the gun that best fits you and your intended use, but there are some rotten apples in any barrel.

Typically "bad" clerks are only at "bad" gun stores, and those are easy to spot. My general rule is that if the shop doesn't look clean enough that you would be confident eating a sandwich prepared there it's probably a "bad" gun store with nasty clerks and overpriced firearms. Looks may be deceiving and once in a while you find an excellent gun store nestled into a run-down old building (such as my local gun store in San Antonio), but in general my "sandwich" rule applies.

If you do wander into a "bad" gun store remember to be polite and not touch anything without permission. If at any time you feel uncomfortable simply make your way quickly and quietly to the door and skedaddle. Most gun stores operate under increased observation and scrutiny from local law enforcement and city officials, which means that the employees will do everything in their power to keep a crime from being committed on the premises. So at the very least you shouldn't be risking any bodily harm by walking into a "bad" shop. In theory. Like I said, trust your instincts and don't go anywhere you're not comfortable.

One thing you may instantly notice when walking in the door is that most gun stores have a Republican or conservative outlook in terms of politics. My favorite gun store here in Virginia has a television on over the cash register that has Fox News playing constantly and Republican campaign stickers plastered on the walls. Being raised a New York Democrat I may not see eye-to-eye with them on many issues but as soon as we start talking about guns the differences we have don't matter anymore. Gun store employees typically have a passion for firearms and anyone who expresses an interest in their passion will be met with friendliness and an eagerness to help find the right gun.

One final drawback of "bad" gun stores is that they may take their conservative stereotype a little too seriously. Racism, sexism and intolerance towards those with alternate sexual orientations have all been encountered at such shops. It's a shame, as those are often the populations which are most in need of self-protection. While I've never been one to suggest backing down in the face of a bully I will recommend that when planning to visit a gun store you make an effort not to draw attention to any quirks that a typical conservative may take opposition to, such as wearing shirts with political statements on them or dressing and acting in a provocative manner. Some gun stores will be tolerant of the views of others (I've taken a liking to walking into the local store with my Obama 2012 shirt) but that's not something worth risking on the first trip. And, like I said, be ready to head for the hills at the first sign of trouble.

The best option for finding a "good" gun store is to get recommendations. The local shooting range will be filled with people who can recommend a good gun store, local message boards will also have that information, and if all else fails armsdealer.net is a fantastic resource available on the internet. Calling in advance is another good way to gauge how you will be treated in the store, as clerks that talk down to you and speak dismissively on the phone will not likely be much better in person, and finding out before you ever set foot in the store can save you time, frustration and gas money.

At the Shooting Range

There is nothing so much like God on earth as a Range Officer on his firing line.

A shooting range can be a dangerous place. It's a space where people go to use explosives and other reactive chemicals which propel small pieces of metal very, very fast. And while fatal accidents do happen at ranges, statistically speaking you're more likely to be injured or killed driving to the range than at the range itself. The way people keep ranges so safe is through the use of a common set of operating procedures and one person – the Range Safety Officer (RSO) – who is in charge of all operations on that range.

The Range Officer is often a paid employee of the range but can also be a volunteer. Any and all commands given by the range officer must be obeyed immediately. It's their range; you're just someone they are allowing to use it temporarily. Following the commands of the Range Officer will keep you safe, and disobeying them has a tendency to result in law enforcement officers being called in to "handle" the situation. In short, listen to what they're telling you and don't piss them off.

When you get to the shooting range you should figure out if you need to check in somewhere and pay a range fee of some sort. Some ranges are free and open to the public, but most charge a fee that helps pay for maintenance. Be polite and ask for a lane on the firing line, and don't be surprised if they make you fill out a waiver or sign some acknowledgement that you have read their range rules and agree to abide by them.

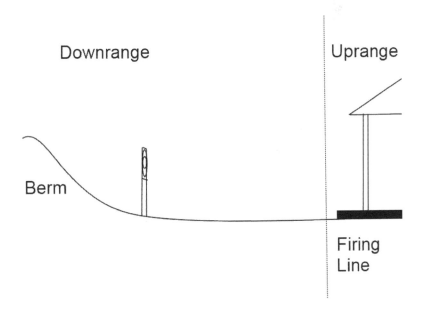

Shooting ranges generally have these components:

- The **Firing Line** is either a physical or imaginary line running from one end of the range to the other parallel to the targets.
- The **Berm** is a large earth or synthetic barricade built at the far end of the firing range. The Firing Line runs parallel to the berm but at the opposite end of the range. On a football field, for example, the firing line could be the goal line of one end zone and

a berm could be built within the end zone on the opposite side of the field. The idea is that every bullet fired by a shooter on the firing line should impact the berm in an effort to keep the bullets from escaping the confines of the firing range and possibly injuring someone.

- The firing line is divided into **Firing Positions** which are often numbered and have corresponding targets or target holders placed between the firing line and the berm. Each shooter (or group of shooters) is assigned a single firing position. Firing positions usually include a bench or table of some sort.
- **Downrange** is the term for everything between the firing line and the berm, the place where bullets fly. You do not want to be downrange when the line is hot.
- **Uprange** is everything from the firing line back, in the opposite direction of the berm. Everything with a pulse should be uprange while guns are being fired.

Ranges have two "states" which describe the actions permitted by the attendees.

- **Hot** – This state means that the shooters on the firing line may load their weapons and fire at their targets.
- **Cold** – This state means that all firearms must be unloaded and placed on the table or ground. No one may touch a firearm while the range is "cold," even if simply transporting a firearm from the table to your car. The exception is that unloaded firearms may be transported with the permission of the Range Officer.

Most ranges alternate between periods of being "hot" and "cold" to allow for people to go downrange and set up their targets. Some ranges have removed the requirement to go downrange by installing electronic targets or moveable target frames that allow shooters to adjust their targets without ever going downrange. Such ranges are perpetually in a "hot" state, meaning you can never go downrange and anyone can fire at any time. Ranges that are run continuously "hot" will let you know before you begin.

In order to facilitate the movement between states, the Range Officer will often give a series of commands. Here's the progression of the range commands aboard Marine Corps Base Quantico, going from a cold range to a hot range and back again.

- **Is the line ready?** – This command is the signal that the range officer is getting ready to declare the range "hot." At this point you should look around and make sure there's no one downrange. Make sure to stand well behind the firing line.
- **Ready on the right? Ready on the left? All ready on the firing line!** – This time they're actually asking you a question. If you see something unsafe (a dog running around by the targets, someone having a picnic on the berm) speak up.
- **With eye and ear protection in place you may load and make ready!** – This is the signal to don your eye protection and hearing protection and get into position. At this point you may load your firearms but you CANNOT fire yet. Some ranges skip this step.
- **You may commence fire, the line is HOT!** – NOW you can pull that trigger.
- **Five minute warning!** – A good Range Safety Officer will give you advanced notice of when they intend to go "cold" so you can finish whatever you're doing and start to unload your firearm.
- **Cease fire, cease fire, cease fire on the line!** – Technically anyone can say this command at any time. If at any time you see something unsafe yell it out. When you hear "cease fire" IMMEDIATELY stop shooting, unload your firearm, place it on the bench or on the ground and step back.
- **Actions open, magazines out, and step back from the firing line** – The RSO is prompting you to show him a "clear" weapon with no ammunition anywhere in it. Be sure to step a good 3 feet behind the firing line and do not handle any firearms. Sometimes they

will actually inspect every firearm on the firing line, but more often they will just glance up and down the line.

- **The line is cold, you may go downrange and adjust your targetry!** – The RSO is now satisfied that it is safe for you to go downrange. I always like to take one last look to my left and right before I step forward of the line just in case there's some idiot the RSO missed, but in general all should be well.

Some ranges don't have range officers assigned to them, such as ranges on public land. In this case you need to be extra attentive to your surroundings and other shooters to ensure that everyone leaves with their blood on the inside. Communicate with your fellow shooters when you want to go downrange to post targets or adjust them, and ensure that everyone knows the range is cold and has put their guns down before you go downrange. An unmanaged range such as this can be intimidating for a new shooter but as long as you communicate you should be fine.

If at any time you feel uncomfortable at the range LEAVE IMMEDIATELY. As I keep saying, you and you alone are responsible for your safety. Putting yourself in a dangerous situation is a great way to get yourself hurt, and there are ALWAYS other ranges.

Here are the typical rules of a firing range:

- No one can go forward of this line without permission from the Range Officer, and only if no one else on the line is handling or firing a firearm AND the range is "cold."
- Only shooters who are about to fire a weapon should be on the firing line, everyone else should be about 1-2 yards behind them.
- All weapons should be unloaded unless they are on the firing line and about to be fired.
- All weapons should have their actions "open" when not in use and have all detachable magazines removed.
- All rounds fired must impact the berm.

- You may only fire at your own target.
- Fire at a slow pace, firing one round every 1-2 seconds. If you want to fire faster ask permission from the RSO.
- Eye and hearing protection are required at all times by all mammals.
- Pregnant women and animals are not allowed (due to lack of hearing protection for the fetus and animals).

Remember to always ask before doing something if you're not sure whether it's allowed at that range, and if you ever have a question about something feel free to ask. Generally the people you find at a firing range are some of the nicest people you'll ever meet and they're more than happy to help you.

<u>Articles for Further Reading</u>

One of my favorite side jobs is as a writer for the website The Truth About Guns. I'm the resident firearms facts, math and statistics guru and have a running segment called "Ask Foghorn" where readers submit questions and I get the opportunity to pontificate on an answer. A couple of these articles are ideal reading material for new shooters and offer some good advice, and so I've slotted them here in the back in case you (the reader) were interested.

Ask Foghorn: Should I buy an AK or AR? Which is better?

A reader writes:

[Should I b]uy an[..] AR or an AK? If an AK, any suggestions?

Man, you just opened a can of worms. And I've got a crowbar to open it even further. Let's get this thing rolling.

There's a popular table out there from 7.62x54r.net that I'd like to use to start the conversation. There's another column about the Mosin Nagant, but that's another story for another day.

Stuff you know if you have an AK	Stuff you know if you have an AR
It works though you have never cleaned it. Ever.	You have $9 per ounce special non-detergent synthetic Teflon infused oil for cleaning.
You are able to hit the broad side of a barn from inside.	You are able to hit the broad side of a barn from 600 meters.
You can put a .30" hole through 12" of oak, if you can hit it.	You can put one hole in a paper target at 100 meters with 30 rounds.
You can intimidate your foe with the bayonet mounted.	You foes laugh when you mount your bayonet.
Your rifle can be used by any two bit nation's most illiterate conscripts to fight elite forces worldwide.	Your rifle is used by elite forces worldwide to fight two bit nations' most illiterate conscripts.

The AR-15 and the AK-47 (I know there are variants, we're using the generic name here) were born out of two very different societies with very different cultures, and had two very different design goals. They fill a similar role, but these differences mean that each weapon has its own strengths and weaknesses and may be better or worse suited to the task in mind. C. J. Chiver's book The Gun does a fantastic job of going into those differences in great detail, but I'll give a quick synopsis.

The AK-47 was designed by a post-WWII Soviet Union. They had just suffered through over a half a decade of warfare where the use of poorly trained conscripts in large numbers proved to be a winning tactic. Guns like the Mosin Nagant and PPS-43, which were simple to use and maintain and could be readily mass produced on basic equipment, provided that capability. Even the most uneducated Ukrainian peasant could be taught how to operate them quickly and efficiently. The AK-47 was a continuation of that design principle, creating a weapon that was easy to produce in large numbers, virtually maintenance-free and easy to operate.

The Soviet experience from WWII taught them that close quarters street to street fighting was going to be the focus of the next great war. Events like Stalingrad and the Battle for Berlin taught them that the long and accurate Mosin Nagant was too big to maneuver effectively (hence the shortened M38 and M44) and overpowered for typical combat distances. By the end of the war it was not uncommon for entire units of soldiers to be armed with only PPS-43 submachine guns due to their effectiveness at close range. The close distance relieved some of the need for accurate fire, meaning that tolerances could be looser and production made easier.

The ammunition chosen for this new firearm was the 7.62×39 round. The 7.62 caliber bullet provided adequate penetration and meant that the same machinery used to manufacture other weaponry (such as basically everything produced since 1891) could be used to manufacture barrels and bullets for the new gun. The shorter case, 39mm instead of 54mm, meant that less powder and brass would be needed for each round and the recoil would be more manageable in fully automatic fire.

Americans have always had an infatuation with accuracy at distance. Marine Corps — I rest my case. The U.S. Army had come to some of the same conclusions as the Soviets about WWII, specifically that engagements took place at short range and that fully automatic weapons were the way forward, but were unwilling to relinquish the idea of the American Rifleman. The ideal rifle and cartridge, they dictated, needed to reliably penetrate the helmet of an enemy soldier at 500 yards. Eugene Stoner and ArmaLite developed such a weapon, using the same machined aluminum that they used (until then) for airplane parts. The result was an accurate and lightweight weapon that was adopted by the U.S. Air Force as the XM16E1 and later the M16.

The ammunition chosen for this new firearm was the 5.56x45mm cartridge. U.S. Army testing indicated that, at high velocity, a .22 caliber bullet would have the same equivalent power as a 7.62 round but drastically reduce the weight of the ammunition required to be carried by soldiers. The smaller cartridge drastically reduced recoil and the materials needed to produce each round while maintaining a penetration capability to the satisfaction of the U.S. Army.

Initially, the M16 (AR-15) had issues with reliability. This was due to a mixture of bad ammunition, shoddy production on Colt's part, and poor maintenance in the field. It wasn't the soldier's fault — early XM16E1s were issued without cleaning kits and touted as never needing to be cleaned. The failures took a toll on soldier's lives and led to a congressional investigation. Modern AR-15s fixed these issues with chrome lining and proper finishing but still remain sensitive to wear and tear.

Yes, they do (preemptive rebuttal). Have you ever seen an AK complain that its gas piston is 1/100th of an inch too short? No. But I've seen an AR do that with its gas rings. So there.

71

OK, that's interesting, but which is better?

Heh, nice try. I'm not falling for that trap.

The different environments in which the guns were designed mean that the two rifles fill two very different roles. Let's compare and contrast some of these differences, perhaps in a chart-like manner.

	AK-47	AR-15
Ammunition	Heavy	Light
Bullet Penetration	Deep	Shallow
Accuracy	Low	High
Weight	Heavy	Light
Recoil	Heavy	Light
Ergonomics	Poor	Good
Reliability	High	Low
Cleaning	Easy	Hard
Maintenance	Hard	Easy
Cost	Cheap	Expensive

It's a simplification of the facts, but it gets the point across. All values are relative to the other weapon and are binary, there is no "middle ground." Cost, by the way, includes ammunition and cleaning costs.

I just want to take a second and explain the one thing I know people are going to get pissed off at: the maintenance and cleaning rows. "Cleaning"

I determined based on how fast and how easy it is to field strip the weapon, which the AK takes the cake. Maintenance, on the other hand, is decidedly difficult with an AK where the main components are riveted or welded together. On the AR platform the entire thing can be taken apart and put back together with a screwdriver, a large hammer and a wrench.

The idea of one being "best," though, depends on what you want it for. To give you an example, here are a couple case studies.

Case study 1: Alice

Alice is a college student. She has a little bit of money (enough to buy a new gun) but income is slow, so cheap is good. She wants a semi-automatic magazine fed rifle for home defense as well as "zombie preparedness," but mainly imagines using it at the local 50-yard range. She doesn't have the cash for fancy upgrades or expensive parts, all she needs is a gun that can run cheaply

Alice's best option is the AK-47 or one of its variants. The short ranges at which it will be used, plus the added mass of the bullets make it ideal for home defense, zombie eradication or use at the relatively short range he has at his disposal. Also, because she's a lazy college kid she's not as likely to clean her gun so the AK's dirt tolerant action is perfect for her.

Case Study 2: Bob

Bob is a young man with a steady job. Not a very well paying one, but steady, so a big investment isn't an issue. He wants a semi-automatic magazine fed rifle for use in 3-gun competitions and varmint hunting at longer distances. He expects to be able to buy some fancy gadgets for his gat down the line.

For Bob, the AR-15 is the ideal weapon. His targets are a little further away than Alice's, and require much less force to penetrate. Plus, lighter ammunition and recoil will help Bob in his 3-gun competitions.

OK, so really now. Which is better?

There you go again trying to make me choose one.

Which one is best for you really depends on your planned use. Close-in fighting for cheap bastards really belongs to the AK-47, while long range engagement for those who want accessories really is the domain of the AR-15.

In the end, shooter's preference rules the day. But I've owned both, and I like both. Just for different reasons. Here are my personal opinions on the matter:

- **AK-47:** Mechanically fascinating, satisfying to work the action, recoil is fun, no need for improvement and runs like a Swiss clock forever.

- **AR-15:** Precision instrument, low recoil, low weight, tons of accessories, easy to swap out parts, ergonomic.

Fine. Both are great guns. But which do you recommend?

Finally, a good question and one that I'm happy to answer. Neither rifle is necessarily "better," but I do have a personal preference.

In my personal opinion the fact that an AR-15 is lightweight, low recoil and highly accurate makes it the superior choice. The platform also allows the shooter to change calibers either with a new upper or a conversion kit, and can be made to fire the extremely cheap .22lr round. The high customizability of the gun also makes it very appealing, as it can be molded to fit your exact need. A little extra investment up front can make all the difference.

In Short: If you can only buy one magazine fed semi-automatic rifle and are on the fence, get an AR-15. But if you're leaning towards one or the other go with your heart and you won't be disappointed.

Ask Foghorn: Best AR-15 for First Time Black Rifle Owners

John writes:

I want to buy my first black rifle. I have decided on a Colt SP6920. I'd buy a LE6920 but I don't feel like paying an extra $200.00 for some roll marks. I have an opportunity to buy one from an established gun seller outside the southeastern PA area for around a thousand bucks or so.

My questions: Would you recommend any gun other than the 6920 as my first AR style rifle? Do you like the 6920? Is $1,000.00 to $1,100.00 for a new one a decent price?

This is actually a very well timed question — I just put together a new "bare bones" AR build a few weeks ago to use as a guinea pig for TTAG reviews. Let's take a couple minutes and discuss the best options for those with a hankering for an evil black rifle.

While an AR-15 seems like a complicated piece of machinery to the uninitiated, in reality it probably couldn't be any simpler. That feature makes it perfect for first time owners of semi-automatic firearms, along with the ease of maintenance, low recoil, abundance of accessories, light weight... I think you get the point.

That relatively simple design means that those looking to purchase a new AR-15 have some options available that tend to lower the price of the gun. When obtaining a new AR-15, the prospective owner can:

- Buy a complete new firearm

- Buy a complete used firearm

- Build the firearm from scratch

- Build the lower and buy the upper complete

Each of these options have benefits and drawbacks, but I do think there is a clear winner (for me, at least).

The first and most obvious option is to buy the firearm already fully assembled. The main benefits are that the firearm doesn't require any additional assembly, can be used immediately, and is guaranteed to work. For new owners this is the easiest option to choose and probably your safest bet, but it probably won't be cheap.

Brand new AR-15 rifles can cost a pretty penny, usually in the $1,000 – $1,500 range. The Colt SP6920 indicated by our reader seems to be going for around $1,043, which is right around the normal price for a complete gun. So in answer to the reader's last question yes, $1,000 is an OK price for that specific model.

While the Colt may be a little pricey, those who value their dollars over a name brand have some options. For example, DS Arms has a DSA Z4 Carbine for $759.95 that has almost every feature the Colt sports. Spike's

Tactical has another similar rifle, their ST-15, for $849. Bushmaster takes the cake with their M4A1 rifle, weighing in at a stunningly low $699 (and lacks iron sights). Olympic Arms also has an offering for $599, but it's nowhere near what our reader wanted. In short, there are options.

The main difference (for new shooters, at least) between these alternative rifles is the rollmark. Every AR-15 is stamped with the manufacturer's name, location and the firearm's serial number and caliber, but some companies also press on a design to make the rifles more appealing. I'm a huge fan of the original Colt rollmark from the M16A1 days, but not enough of a fan to spend the extra cash just to get that design on my gun.

Rollmarks are the big visual difference, but these guns also vary wildly in terms of quality and reliability. If I were buying a new rifle the Spike's Tactical would be very appealing because I've used their equipment before and I like them, but I'd be weary of Bushmaster thanks to their recent colossal failure with the ACR. Colt has a great reputation, and if you're willing to pay out the dollars it might not be a bad idea.

Option #2 is to buy the gun used. Sure it doesn't have that "new gun smell," but theoretically you can get higher quality parts for the same amount of dosh. Theoretically. In reality, the asking price for even the crappiest ARs are only around 10% discounted. While the supply is gigantic, the demand for these rifles is even bigger. If you want to go the "used" route the best idea is to avoid Gunbroker at all costs and try to find the relevant local gun trading forum for your state. Pennsylvania has PAFOA, Virginia has VA Gun Trader, Maryland has MD Shooters, the list goes on. Private party transfers provide the best chance for getting a good deal on your new gun.

Option #3 gives the owner the opportunity to save some money by assembling the gun themselves and lets them pick out exactly what they want in their rifle by building it from scratch. This option provides the highest level of customization, but also requires a good bit of mechanical skill. And a vice.The mechanical thing, not alcohol. Although some of us have that too.

Building an AR-15 from scratch really only requires a few major purchases: upper receiver, bolt carrier assembly, lower receiver, barrel, handguards, stock, parts kit. There's a couple other minor parts involved but they're all $10 or less. In theory this can yield a complete rifle for around $600 – $700, but in reality you're still going to end up paying close to $800.

The last option (#4), and the one I actually recommend, is to build the lower receiver and buy the upper complete. One of the unique features of the AR-15 platform is that the gun is composed of two interchangeable parts — an upper and lower receiver. Of these parts, the more important to how well a gun feels is the lower receiver as it contains the stock, the grip and the trigger.

Building the lower from parts only requires a hammer, a screwdriver and a place to work, and the process can be done in under an hour. While putting all the pieces together may seem daunting, the major benefit from doing it yourself is the knowledge gained about how the gun works and the knowledge of how to service the firearm and improve it later on.

Another giant benefit of building the lower from parts is the ability to choose your own rollmark. If you want a cheap lower (and don't mind being a billboard) lowers can be had for as little as $74.99. On the other side of the scale "specialty" lowers can run anywhere from $150 – $50,000 (for machine guns, that is). Any lower will do if all you care about is semi-automatic fun, but choosing a rollmark that looks great is something that I find appealing and an easy way to "pimp" your gun a little.

Building a good lower will cost around $450, and an OK lower can be around $250-300 for the bare bones features. Once that is built you can select your very own upper in whatever caliber strikes your fancy, the most popular being 5.56, 5.45, .22lr and .300 BLK. Some can be had for only $399 with almost exactly the same profile as the colt indicated in the question.

That was a bit of a long answer to a relatively short question, so let me try to sum this up:

- **Would you recommend any gun other than the 6920 as my first AR style rifle?** The Colt SP6920 is as good an AR-15 as any other model. It has all the features I look for in a carbine length AR and should serve you well in recreational shooting or even 3-gun competitions. But there are other similar options available for less money.

- **Do you like the 6920?** Never fired it, but it looks OK to me. Colt has a great track record (recently) with firearms and AR-15s in particular, so if you hear your heart calling for one I wouldn't resist.

- **Is $1,000.00 to $1,100.00 for a new one a decent price?** Decent? Yes. But there are cheaper options as well.

At the end of the day any of these options will get you a new AR-15 for about the same price, give or take $300ish. I prefer to build my own lowers from parts because I like to be able to select which components I use, but it's a personal preference thing. Your own level of mechanical skill and desire to customize will drive which path forward you choose. But thanks to the high level of parts interchangeability and the ease of use whatever AR-15 you ultimately buy will be OK, or you can quickly make it OK by changing a few parts.

Ask Foghorn: Best AK-47 for First Time Commie Milsurp Owners?

Reader Texan asks:

In line with your previous article (Best AR-15 for First Time Black Rifle Owners), what is a good AK-47 for the first time AK-er?

The AK-47 system is the most popular firearm ever produced no matter what metric you use. Firearms produced, worldwide ownership, countries that issue it to their troops — Mozambique even has it prominently displayed on its flag. As with any popular firearm, many different configurations have been developed to fill different roles, but for a first time buyer the choice is obvious. Before we get to that, let's talk a little bit about the design and history of the AK-47.

The original design for the AK-47 was as a replacement for the main battle rifle of the Soviet Union. They wanted something with the portability and rate of fire of a PPS-43, but "stopping power" and penetration comparable to the MosinNagant m1891/30. Intermediate steps like the SVT-40 and the SKS proved useful in combat, but the predominantly wood construction and relatively intricate machining required for such guns made production on a large scale problematic.

The AK-47, designed mostly by a team led by Mikhail Kalashnikov (but integrating parts from other competing designs as well), was the ideal weapon for the Soviet Union. The simple metal receiver and parts meant that they could be turned out in great numbers and required fewer raw materials than previous weapons, the operation was so simple that Ukrainian peasants could be quickly trained on its use, and the extended 30-round magazines (something only seen in machine guns to this point) meant the soldier could be more effective for longer periods of time. An improved version, the AKM, used a stamped instead of a milled receiver and became the most widely produced firearm ever.

The original design, using the 7.62x39mm round, was built in a vast number of different designs and by many different arsenals behind the Iron Curtain. Variants included the RPK (heavy barrel and bipod for machine gun use), AKMS (folding stock for airborne troops), and the AKS (for use in armored vehicles).

After the Vietnam conflict the Soviet powers that be got it into their heads that a .22 caliber projectile was the way to go, seeing the space and weight saving benefits as well as wanting to go with the "modern" trend of firearms development. The AK-47 was redesigned to accept a new cartridge, the 5.45x39mm round, and became known as the AK-74. This "improved" AK would be the weapon of choice for decades to come, a lighter weapon with less recoil and one which was easier to control in fully automatic fire.

In reality, there are two "best" AK pattern rifles because there are two major calibers. For those who want an AK because of the enjoyable recoil of the 7.62x39mm round (or its penetration capability) there's an AK-47 variant, and for someone who wants a fun shooter with cheap ammo that will last a lifetime there's a 5.45x39mm AK-74 variant. Unfortunately (or fortunately?) the popularity of the AK pattern firearm has meant a massive increase in importation of different kinds and one specific model designation won't be valid for more than a few weeks (while it's in stock). So instead, I'm going to list off the features that a first time AK buyer should look for, no matter what caliber their heart desires.

- **Fixed full stock.** This is probably the most important feature new AK buyers will want. Some AKs come with folding or swinging stocks to make them more useful to troopers in confined spaces, but it makes getting a cheek weld impossible and makes the gun feel terrible. If you really want an underfolding AK stock go for it, but just realize that you might regret it later.

- **Stamped receiver.** Some people prefer milled receivers (machined from a single block of material) but for a first time buyer the weight and cost savings of a stamped receiver outweigh the benefits of a milled receiver. I'm not saying that if you find one for a great price you shouldn't buy it, instead I'm suggesting you focus your search on the more popular stamped variety.

- **Threaded muzzle.** The vast majority of AK pattern rifles came from the factory with some form of threaded muzzle so they could take muzzle brakes and other fun things. Some rifles, like the WASR-10, have a nut "permanently" welded to cover these threads, but that can be removed with a Dremmel. In fact, it may actually be harder to find an AK without a muzzle device. Anyway, I recommend you have one.

- **Side accessory rail.** The AK series rifle often has a funky looking mount on the left side of the receiver. This was designed to allow shooters to quickly add or remove optics from the rifle, including all manner of scopes and red dot sights. The Soviet equivalent of the AR's top rail.

Any AK is better than no AK, but of the AKs I've fired I have four solid recommendations.

- **GP 1975.** This gun, made by CAI and pictured at the top of the article, is a mostly American manufactured version of the AK-47 in 7.62x39mm. It works great, and it's currently running about $420 (cheaper than the imports).

- **Romanian AK-MV / WASR-10.** The Romanian imported AK pattern rifles in 7.62x39mm have historically been of superb quality and low price. The ones my friends have purchased have had the muzzle threads covered by a nut, but that was easy to remove. $450.

- **Arsenal SSGL31.** This Russian made AK-74 pattern rifle in 5.45x39mm has proven to be of excellent quality and beautiful as well. Which is great, because the price tag of $800ish is a little steep. Just make sure you're 922(r) compliant.

- **Polish Tantal AK-74.** There have been some issues with the barrels being of the wrong caliber (5.56 not 5.45), so make sure to check your targets for keyholing. CAI (who assembles them) has been very good about replacing defective guns. It does have a wire folding stock, but at $410 I could live with it.

Almost any gun store sells AKs, but the cheapest place I've found online is J & G Arms. Their low prices and friendly staff have always been helpful to me, so I highly recommend you give them a glance.

Ask Foghorn: Self Defense Shotguns

A reader writes:

I'm a new reader and was wondering if you've ever posted about home defense shotguns and what to look for when purchasing one. If not, would you be able to point me toward a few good resources, or perhaps do a post on this topic at some point in the future? I'm sure I'm not the only one with questions about this.

Personally I can't imagine a better suited firearm for home defense than a handgun. It's compact, accurate, and easy to maneuver around the house. But for some the shotgun is their firearm of choice, requiring less fine motor skill and easier to aim in a high stress situation. So today's question: If I were to get a self defense shotgun, what would it be?

There are certain benefits to a shotgun for home defense. Buckshot is big benefit #1, placing more holes in the target in a shorter period of time and having a greater probability of hitting something vital and stopping the threat. Slugs are the other major benefit, giving not only the ability to hit a target at distance but also easily penetrate some forms of cover (walls, car windshields, etc) and create a massive wound channel. Maximizing these benefits is the key to using a shotgun for a home defense weapon.

Like most things there are a number of companies that have products that meet my criteria. So instead of just listing my ideal home defense shotgun I'm going to rattle off my "wish list" of features that a good home defense shotgun needs to have and you can decide what company makes the right gun for you.

Pump Action

There are hundreds of stories of home intruders being scared away simply by the sound of a pump action shotgun being racked, but that's not the reason it makes my list. Making a loud noise gives away your position to the attacker and is probably one of the last things you want to do (but, if they already know you're there, it wouldn't hurt).

Pump action shotguns have a feature that makes them ideal: reliability. Semi-automatic shotguns may have increased in reliability over the last few years but when my life is on the line I want to know that the action is going to cycle and that next round is going to be loaded, and a pump action is the only type of shotgun that gives me that reliable cycle and can tell me instantly if the round didn't seat. If anything goes wrong with a pump you'll know it well before you try and pull the trigger, possibly saving yourself precious seconds to fix it and stop the threat in time.

Short Barrel

The shorter the better. 18 inches is the legal minimum length for a shotgun without venturing into $200 tax land, but if you have the time and the money it might not be a bad idea to get the stamp and break out the hacksaw.

Long guns have a disadvantage in close quarters situations because they give the attacker something to grab, namely the barrel. As soon as they get hold of the barrel they can make you miss or even try to take the gun out of your hands. That's why I love pistols for close quarters situations — they don't have that problem. Still, if the shotgun is your weapon of choice grab the 18" or 18.5" barrel versions.

Attached Shell Holder

Shotgun ammunition is gigantic. The only thing in my ammo closet that takes up more room is the .50 BMG rounds, and since ArmaLite politely asked me to return their AR-50its going to be sitting there for quite some time. Due to their massive size you can't really load all that many into the gun at one time. So if you get into a protracted gunfight you may very quickly become screwed. The solution is simple: keep extra rounds on the gun.

Why not just have some spare shells strewn about, you say? Because in the middle of the night if something happens where I need my gun I know exactly where it is and exactly where the extra ammo can be found. Keeping both together in one easy to grab package is essential.

The other reason for a shell holder is to take advantage of both buckshot and slugs. Keeping the shotgun loaded with buckshot is a good idea, as if you are attacked you're probably going to need some "close range" power and that's what buckshot is great for. But if your attacker starts shooting at you from a distance you'll need to switch to slugs to engage them, and if you have some distance between you and the attacker you'll have some time to make that swap. The only way you'll have that capability is if (you guessed it) the shells are right there on the gun.

This is a feature that is probably easier to get after you buy the gun than it is to buy from the factory, so don't exclude a shotgun just because it doesn't have this in the box.

Pistol Grip

While the standard shotgun stock will work just fine a pistol grip makes the whole thing a lot more ergonomic. There's no fancy explanation behind this criteria, I just like it. So there.

Full Length Stock

Some people advocate for shotguns that have a pistol grip and then no stock to hold against your shoulder, citing their
increased maneuverability and shorter overall length. But you instantly lose an amazing level of accuracy for the average shooter the second that stock goes away. The full length stock on a shotgun not only gives the shooter more control over the gun during firing but can also be used as a blunt weapon in a worst case scenario.

Ghost Rings

Most shotguns sold use a "bead" sighting system. Sight down the top of the gun, put the bead on the target, and bye bye target. But sometimes you need a little more accuracy, and that's where ghost rings come in.

A ghost ring sight uses a large ring at the back that the shooter looks through and a post in the front that the shooter aligns with the target. Not only are these more accurate than the bead sights but they're often easier to use and faster to acquire than the other types.

I know what you're thinking, and I'm thinking it too. "**Hey Foghorn, it sounds an awful lot like the KSG is your ideal gun.**" But it's not. In the hands of our writers the KSG has proven to be a somewhat finicky shotgun, and the magazine switching capability (while increasing capacity) is one more thing to forget in a gunfight. While on paper a KSG seems like a great idea and the perfect weapon, just like with a number of other Kel-Tec products the quality and reliability often isn't the same as a standard firearm.

If you want to know my ideal shotgun down to the make and model it's a toss-up between the Mossberg 500 SPX and the Remington 870 Express Tactical. Both guns feature close to 18" barrels, pistol grips, and ghost rings installed from the factory. The Mossberg firearm also includes a shell holder in the stock, so that might be something to consider when shopping for your gun.

Ask Foghorn: Best Pistol for Competition Shooting for New Shooters?

A reader writes:

[...] I am interested in getting into some kind of shooting sport. I love the sound of 3 gun however, I am not financially ready for this. [...] It looks like the best and cheapest weapon "pistol" I should look into getting is the new Springfield 5.25 in order to shoot the beginners matches. I've been out of the game for 9 years now, I'm a little rusty. Can you offer any advice on my choice of weapon, "the Springfield 5.25"? Also, can you tell me what type of matches I should look into shooting. As I said, I am not familiar with the names of the different styles of shooting matches. I want to start with a pistol competition first.

I assume he means the Springfield XD(m) 5.25, which is brand new for this year. We'll get to that, but first I want to talk about **what makes a good beginner's competition pistol**, and then **what's the best beginner's competition style**.

Shooting competitions are fun, there's no doubt about that — an adrenaline junkie like myself feels right at home with the other addicts on the range. Competitions also encourage and enhance training and provide a great metric for tracking how well you're shooting has improved. And while you do need some form of firearm to start competing, the nice thing about firearms competitions is that you can use just about any kind of handgun as long as it's safe to fire.

For beginners, especially if they're basing their handgun choice on competition shooting, I like to encourage them to keep a few criteria in mind when making their selection. Competition guns for beginners should have the following qualities:

- **Semi-automatic with removable magazines.** Revolvers are fun to compete with, but getting the basics down first is essential. Semi-autos with magazines are intuitive, easy to load, easy to use, and ergonomic.

- **Chambered in 9mm.** Say what you want about "stopping power," but for beginner shooters the relatively low recoil of the 9mm round, the low expense of the ammunition and the higher capacity of the associated magazines make using it in a competition ideal.

- **"Full Size."** Even if IDPA is your chosen competition a full size handgun will be easier to manipulate and easier to fire. Plus, the longer sight radius will help with accuracy. 4-5 inch barrels are perfect, and anything over 6 starts getting into that "diminishing rate of return" area.

- **Rugged construction.** This one isn't as easy to identify as the other features, but its essential. Competition handguns should be able to handle thousands upon thousands of rounds per year without a problem or any major parts wearing out. If you want to get better practice is the only way, and a firearm that can't handle many long hours on the range isn't any use to us.

- **Ergonomic.** This feature is one each person will have to determine for themselves. For me the biggest reason I use a SIG P226 in competition is that it fits my gigantic bear-like hand so perfectly. A friend of mine uses a 1911 for the same reason, not necessarily because he likes the gun itself. Going to a gun shop and trying out a bunch of different guns is the only way to figure this one out.

- **No manual safety.** This one is going to stick in the craw of the CZ lovers, but a manual safety on a beginner's competition gun is just going to get in the way and confuse them too much. There's a lot going on already when the buzzer goes off, adding one more step to the process of drawing and firing isn't going to help.

A good number of firearms meet the criteria, of which the Springfield XD(m) 5.25 is one. Also in this category are Glock pistols, a good number of SIG SAUER firearms, and some Beretta gats. In short there are a ton of choices, but it's up to you the shooter to decide what works best for you.

As for the Springfield XD(m) 5.25 in particular I haven't had a chance to use it. Yet. So I can't recommend for or against purchasing it. What I do know is that while it costs a pretty penny it does come with almost everything you need to start competing right there in the box (holster, magazines, magazine pouch, gun. If you choose this gun, I again recommend the 9mm flavor.

So what about the best competition style for new competition shooters? The good news is that if you get set up for one you can easily transition into the others. Set up for USPSA? Throw on a jacket and you can do IDPA. Only holster you have is a IWB for IDPA? Works just fine for 3-gun. The required equipment doesn't change much, only the rules and the style. For that reason I would recommend that **the best competition style for new shooters is whatever the local ranges are doing**. No matter what you do, whether its USPSA, IDPA or even Steel Challenge, the people running the match will be more than happy to help you get started and compete for the first time.

BTW, TTAG does have a series of articles explaining some of the competition styles for the uninitiated:

- **USPSA / IPSC** -
  http://www.thetruthaboutguns.com/2011/05/foghorn/competition-shooting-101-uspsa-ipsc/

- **3-Gun** - http://www.thetruthaboutguns.com/2011/04/foghorn/competition-shooting-101-3-gun/

- **CMP / NRA High Power** - http://www.thetruthaboutguns.com/2011/04/foghorn/competition-shooting-101-cmpnra-high-power/

- **IDPA** - http://www.thetruthaboutguns.com/2011/09/foghorn/competition-shooting-101-idpa/

If you have the option, though, I think USPSA would be the ideal competition style to pop your proverbial cherry on. The rules are simple, you can walk the stage before you have to shoot it, and the targets will give you feedback on where you're hitting. The website for USPSA / IPSC also has a handy function that lets you find local clubs that run competitions.

Ask Foghorn: Best Rifle for New Long Distance Shooters

Daniel asks:

> I recently read an article about the mosin nagant, and found it a
> very interesting article. I'm currently learning as much as I can
> about rifles and am looking to purchase one soon, though I'm on a
> highly restricted budget. What attracts me toward the mosin
> nagant is that its incredibly cheap at $90, and I can get 440 rounds
> of it for $70!! In the article, Chris mentions that a modified mosin
> costs around 300, but better more accurate guns can be had for
> the same or less. I was wondering which firearms he was speaking
> of? The main purpose of the gun is not home defense, I want to
> learn basics of long distance marksmanship and use it for hunting
> as well. The chambers had in mind were the 7.62x54r and .308 as I
> believe these rounds are the cheapest for the purpose I'm trying to
> accomplish. Any info would be greatly appreciated. Thanks!

So what you're looking for is a 1,000 yard rifle for $300? Well, let's see
what we can do...

First we need to define the characteristics of a good long distance rifle, and then we can see what's out there that matches our specifications. Keep in mind that these are MY criteria for a good rifle and not THE criteria for a good rifle, so feel free to improvise to suit your own standards. They are, in order...

- **Bolt Action** — There are some people who claim a semi-auto can be just as accurate as a bolt gun, but even they admit that it isn't cheap. It's easier to make an accurate bolt gun than an accurate semi-auto, and so even with the resources of TTAG available to me I still prefer my bolt action rifle for distance shots.

- **Free Floating Barrel** — This is probably the most important feature of the rifle. I've known men to make 1,000 yard shots with iron sights on an AR-15, but I've never known a man to do it without a free floated barrel. Any contact between the stock and the barrel screws up the barrel harmonics and throws the shot off, so make sure Mr. Washington can slide all the way down your barrel.

- **Thirty Cal** — I'm a huge fan of the 7.62×51 / .308 Winchester cartridge. It's one of the most heavily studied and well understood cartridges produced today and provides excellent ballistic properties especially at long range. Plus, it's widely available and relatively cheap.

- **Bull or Target Profile Barrel** — The profile of the barrel describes how thick the material surrounding the bore is. The thicker the material the less likely it is to move between shots and be affected by heat. It's not so important if you don't mind waiting 5 minutes between shots, but it's nice.

- **Scope Mounts** — Usually a bolt action rifle will come with some holes drilled into the receiver so you can get your own rings and mount your scope. Some guns (like the vintrovka Mosina Nagant) don't have this feature and it makes mounting a scope near impossible. Just make sure your gun checks this box.

That's basically my ideal long range rifle. And, oddly enough, I'm testing out that exact setup (well, minus the bull barrel) right now for my 1,000 yard rifle for $500 project. But what other options are out there?

The best option available is to **scour your local classified ads for someone selling their used rifles and buy one that way**. It may be used, but rifles have a long lifespan and buying an older model will let you get a better rifle for your money than you would if you were buying a new one. Plus, the seller will probably be nice enough to let you know how well the rifle works and if it has any quirks you need to know about.

If you've got your heart set on a new rifle, however, there are a few things to be aware of. First is that the most expensive part of the rifle is the barrel profile, and the heavier the profile the more expensive it will be. Short and light barrels are cheap and will work, but they heat up and move quickly. Second, if you buy a new rifle chances are you're going to want a new stock for it fairly soon, so keep in mind that you could be shortly looking at another $100-$200 expense. Just keep those in mind when you're flipping through the gun catalogs.

Here are some rifles I recommend you take a peek at that are right around your price range.

- **Weatherby Vanguard Series 2** — We had our first peek at these rifles at SHOT this year, and despite the slightly out of your price range for MSRP they're going to be my pick for the best choice in bolt action rifles for new long distance shooters. Good enough quality to do the job while still being cheap enough to make some mistakes.

- **Weatherby Vanguard (Old Model)** — Believe it or not there are some new Vanguard rifles still kicking around, despite being a discontinued line. It's actually a benefit now as the price has been decreased to flush them out of the stockrooms, so you can have one for around $300.
- **Ruger American Rifle** — They're a little over your budget, but they're the "new thing" from Ruger and it looks like they've done it properly. I fired one at SHOT and, while not quite a Weatherby, it was definitely head and shoulders above the usual plastic stock bolt gun.
- **Savage Axis** — I've heard good things about the Savage series of rifles, so I'm going to pop it in the list as a recommendation for something to look at. It's a solid gun with a large aftermarket assortment of upgrades should you ever need them.
- **Remington 700** — The Rem 700 is the gold standard for bolt action firearms, and while the quality of manufacturing has gone downhill since Freedom Group took over they still are very accurate rifles.
- **Mossberg 100 ATR** — I briefly owned one and it worked just fine, but I sold it and bought a Weatherby Vanguard in less than 3 months. Just FYI. Still, it's a <2 MoA gun under $300.

IN SHORT, buy a .308 bolt action firearm. Preferably used and locally sourced. It's greener that way.

Ask Foghorn: What Makes a Good Trigger?

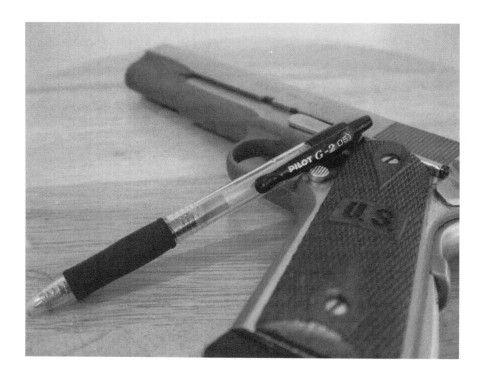

A reader writes:

"It seems people are always complaining about this trigger or that, or talking up the smooth-as-butter qualities of some high-end revolver they've just acquired. I claim almost no idea of what to look for in a trigger, and what idea I can claim comes mostly from reading others wax rhapsodic (or vitriolic) about triggers they've known and loved (or didn't). I'd love to see some relatively clue-fulTTAGer 'splain it all to me."

Quick disclaimer: this article will detail what I think makes a good trigger. Opinions vary wildly depending on what you're doing, what you're shooting, and even personal preference. But the general consensus seems to be that a clean, crisp trigger makes life behind a gun—any gun—just that little bit better.

Before we start talking about how different triggers feel we need a standard frame of reference, which is where the retractable ballpoint pen comes in. Everyone, even people who have never held a gun, have clicked a clicky pen and knows what that feels like. The click of a clicky pen is the worst single stage trigger you can possibly find, and a perfect starting point.

Go on, grab one right now. Click the top a couple of times. You'll notice that there are four distinct stages to the click: the long push, the click, the post-click downward travel, and the reset back to the top. I've always heard these referred to as the "**slack**," the "**break**," the "**overtravel**" and the "**reset**," but they may have other names as well. We'll use this vocabulary to talk about triggers.

On rifles, there are two styles of triggers: single stage and two stage.

Single stage triggers are where the trigger presents a single, continuously increasing point of resistance to the shooter's finger before the "break" releases the trigger. Single stage triggers should have no discernable "slack" before the break.

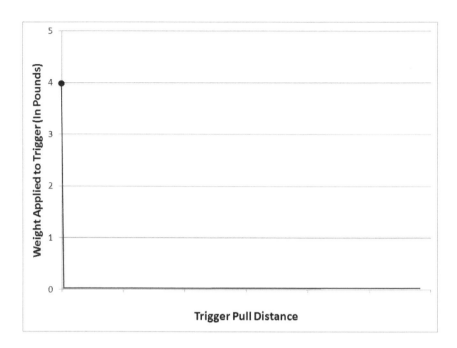

These graphs will help us visualize what triggers feel like. The horizontal axis represents the distance traveled by the trigger as it moves backwards (from left to right), and the vertical axis represents the force required to move past that point on the trigger. The "break" is visualized by a large black dot.

On a "good" single stage trigger like the one in the graph above, there is no slack before the break (the trigger does not move until enough pressure is applied to move past the break). With a good single stage trigger the shooter simply applies constantly increasing pressure until the trigger breaks and doesn't have to worry about taking up any slack before the break.

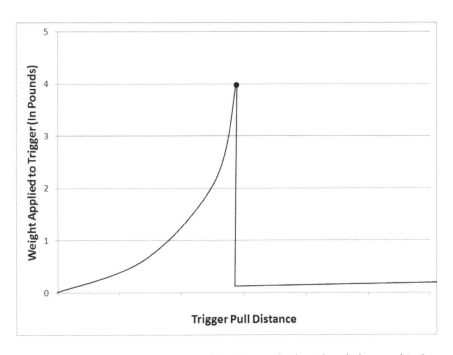

Trigger Pull Distance

(y-axis label) Weight Applied to Trigger (In Pounds)

This is what my old DPMS trigger felt like, and what the clicky pen kinda feels like. As you increase pressure on the trigger, the trigger moves backwards. This backwards movement in a single stage trigger is called "creep," so named because the trigger will usually start and stop moving a couple of times as you apply more pressure, "creeping" backwards to the break rather than in one fluid motion. What makes this kind of trigger difficult to use is that all of the "false starts" with the creeping may encourage the shooter to anticipate the recoil (they think they passed the break when in fact there is more trigger yet to pull).

Two stage triggers are designed to have a certain amount of slack in the beginning of the pull. As the shooter takes up all that slack, the trigger moves backwards for a short distance before hitting stiff resistance. Once the shooter hits this "wall" of resistance the trigger more or less functions like a single stage trigger.

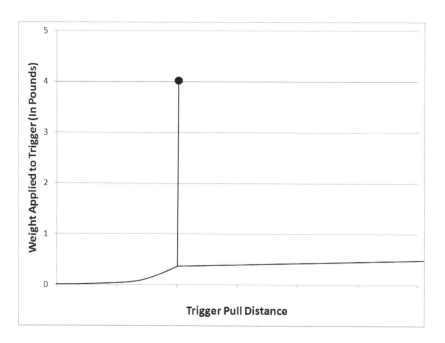

This is what a "good" two stage trigger should feel like. Kinda. My photoshop skills aren't quite up to snuff, but you get the idea. The trigger moves for a bit with a little pressure, then hits the resistance of the second stage and from here the thing acts as a single stage trigger.

Two stage triggers are more common in precision rifle builds than single stage triggers for two reasons. First, the break in the trigger can be comparatively lighter than a single stage trigger. For example, if it takes two pounds of pressure to get the trigger TO the break, then the break itself can be only two pounds of extra force (for a 4 pound trigger). Less force means less jerking and better shot placement. Second, the shooter knows exactly where the break is and can use the slack to make sure they're getting the perfect trigger pull every time. I'm sure there are better reasons, but that's how I use my two stage triggers.

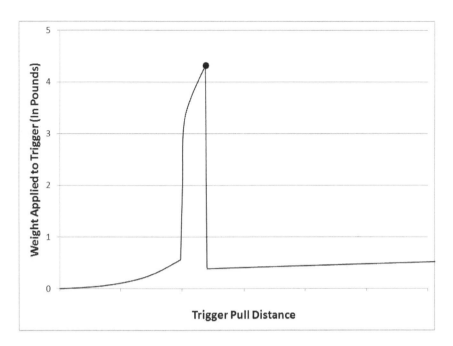

A "bad" two stage trigger will completely negate the reason you bought a two stage trigger in the first place. If the purpose for having a two stage trigger is knowing where the break is, then a "creepy" two stage trigger is not what you want. Creep, as we discussed previously, hides where that break is and makes for some bad habits and bad shots down the road.

On pistols, you either have single action or double action triggers, and they can behave differently depending on the pistol. My SIG, for example, has a single action trigger that feels like a good two stage trigger. My Nagant m1891's single action trigger, on the other hand, is a single stage trigger.

In either case, double action typically should feel like a heavier two stage trigger, with a very strong "slack" period before hitting that "break." A double action trigger should require a constantly increasing amount of pressure, followed by a quick "wall" for a second stage, and then a crisp break. I've heard revolvers that do this exceptionally well called a "butter" pull, but "silky" or "smooth" is equally applicable. Smooth and consistent is the key.

So what is a "crisp" trigger? A crisp or sharp or clean trigger is one that has as little "creep" as possible. As I said in my Timney trigger review, imagine breaking off the tip of an icicle. There should be no hesitation when it breaks, and no "creep" beforehand.

Ask Foghorn: Trigger Terminology

A reader writes:

"trigger's a bit gritty and prone to stacking" Educate me, please. What is stacking?

One of the major problems with talking about guns is that you're often trying to convey a feeling with words. Having a common lexicon (standard set of words with known definitions) helps, but only if you're "in the know." We went over some of these terms in the previous article, but today's Ask Foghorn will try to hit them all. If there's one I missed (or, more likely, one I got wrong) shoot me an email and I'll add it to the list or fix it.

Blade

The "blade" of the trigger is the exposed portion to which the shooter applies pressure to fire the gun.

Break

The "break" of a trigger is the point at which the mechanism releases the hammer (or other mechanism that stores potential energy) to hit the firing pin and strike the primer. It is after this point that the firing of the round is out of the shooter's control — the round is fired and gone, and there's nothing that can stop it. Well, except the backstop, of course.

The "break" can feel either crisp or soft depending on the shooter's preference. Crisp triggers are typically preferred on rifles, where the trigger remains stationary until enough pressure has built up for it to release the firing pin. Soft triggers (or "roll triggers") can sometimes be preferred by competition pistol shooters, which allows the trigger to continue to move backwards while the pressure is building.

Double Action

This term is typically applied to pistols, but it can also be found in other weapons (like the M32 MGL). Unlike a single action trigger, a double action trigger will move the hammer on the firearm backwards, imparting enough potential energy to strike the firing pin and ignite the round, and will also release the hammer once enough energy is stored. This is accomplished in one long, heavy pull to the rear.

Gritty

In contrast to a "smooth" trigger, a "gritty" trigger feels as though the metal trigger is sliding over a rough surface. The force required to pull the trigger may not consistently increase, and will often result in a trigger having properties that are referred to as "stacking."

Over-Travel

Any rearwards movement of the trigger after the "break" is considered "over-travel." The further the over-travel, the further the trigger finger must move forward in order to allow the trigger to "reset." Excessive over-travel and reset distances may fatigue a trigger finger, especially in high round count situations (competition shooting, for example) and lowers the rate of fire for semi-automatic rifles.

Doug wrote in with a quick addition:

In your definition of overtravel, you missed what I feel is probably the most important point about it. The more of it there is, the greater the chance that it will cause the sights to be jerked off target when you come to the end of it.

Reach

The "reach" of a trigger is measured as the distance from the front of the trigger (where your finger would apply pressure) to the front of the grip (behind the trigger). This is essentially a measure of how far forward the trigger is from the grip, which allows you to figure out if your finger is the proper size to manipulate it correctly.

Reset

After the "break," any further rearward movement of the trigger would be useless. There's nothing left for the trigger to do — it has performed its function. To make the gun shoot again, once the cycling of the action is complete the trigger must be "reset." Resetting the trigger is usually no more complicated than allowing it to return to its most forward position, which will re-engage the mechanism to which it is attached. Once re-engaged, the trigger will once again be able to cause a round to be fired. The trigger is usually pushed back into place automatically by an internal spring, and all the operator needs to do is release any pressure on the trigger and cycle the action (if not semi-automatic).

Set

A trigger may sometimes be referred to as a "set" trigger. These triggers give the shooter the option to greatly decrease the force required to pull the trigger past the "break" without breaking out the screwdriver and tearing down the rifle. Sets are usually engaged via a mechanism that is easy to manipulate while the shooter has his sights on a target.

A Single Set trigger means the shooter applies force to the back of the trigger in order to engage the set. This (rather counter-intuitively) moves the trigger further forwards, in the opposite direction that one normally pulls a trigger.

A Double Set trigger requires the shooter to manipulate a lever or catch somewhere on the gun other than the trigger to engage the set. Within set triggers, there are two types or "phases." Single Phase set triggers require the set to be engaged before the trigger can be pulled. Double Phase triggers can be fired either with or without engaging the set. Phases are most common on Double Set triggers.

Shoe

A "trigger shoe" is like putting a veneer on your trigger. It's a piece of material that is affixed to the blade of the trigger in order to make it wider or change some other characteristic of the trigger. Shoes are not typically permanent.

Single Action

A "single action" trigger is one where the only function of the trigger is to release the hammer (or other mechanism that stores potential energy) and enables it to strike the firing pin. That's it. If the hammer (or mechanism) is already forward and has no potential energy then pulling the trigger will not do anything (unlike a "double action" trigger). Single action triggers are usually much lighter than double action triggers, and do not move backwards until after the "break."

Single Stage

See "single stage" in the previous Ask Foghorn for more detail, but essentially the trigger does not move until the pressure is sufficient for it to "break."

Slack

The "slack" is the distance that the trigger moves backwards before resistance is felt. On a two stage trigger it is this slack that comprises the first stage. Slack in a single stage trigger is usually considered a very bad thing. See the previous Ask Foghorn for more information.

Smooth

A "smooth" trigger is the opposite of a "gritty" trigger. When pulling a smooth trigger to the rear it will present a constantly increasing level of resistance (or simply constant resistance in a single stage trigger) and will feel like two smooth and oiled pieces of metal sliding across each other. Smooth triggers will not "stack."

Stacking

A trigger that has "stacking" issues will have an area of unintentionally increased resistance before the "break." This can also be referred to as a "false break." In a trigger that has stacking issues the shooter needs to apply enough pressure to get past the "stack," which is usually enough to move past the "break" as well once the "stack" has been passed. This means that it's more difficult to control the firearm for precision shots.

Stop

The stop is a physical object (typically a piece of metal machined into the trigger or an adjustable screw) that limits the over-travel of the trigger. The stop will literally stop the trigger from moving any further backwards.

Two Stage

A "two stage" trigger, unlike a single stage trigger, has a bit of "slack" built into the trigger. The shooter takes up the slack in the trigger by applying a small amount of pressure to the trigger. Once the slack is taken up, the trigger is at the "break" location and only needs a small further increase in pressure to fire the weapon. Two stage triggers are useful especially in precision rifles because once the slack is taken up it only requires a very small amount of pressure to fire the gun, less than would be required (or safe) in a single stage trigger.

The Truth about the AR-15 Rifle

In the wake of the post-Sandy Hook media frenzy, it's unfortunate that the vast majority of pundits have no idea what they're talking about when it comes to guns. Especially with a firearm like the AR-15 (often referred to as the "Assault Rifle"). Scanning the press coverage, there's no end of misinformation about the ArmaLite Rifle (AR) design and why it is such a popular firearm in the United States. Hopefully I can put some of that right. So, if you're looking for the real reasons why the AR-15 is an insanely popular firearm, here are the top three:

1.Versatility

Before the AR-15 rifle made its way onto the market gun owners needed to buy a different gun for each caliber and application.

Whether they wanted inexpensive target shooting (with cheap ammo like .22lr) or deer hunting (with a more substantial caliber like .308

Winchester), owners had to buy a different firearm for each use. Changing calibers was expensive, time consuming, and generally a one-way process.

Shooters were also stuck with their rifle's ergonomics. If the stock was too long or too short there wasn't much they could do—except pay a gunsmith to modify the gun. The same was true if you didn't like the rifle's trigger or the sights. Changing anything was a major pain in the butt.

With an AR-15, gun owners don't need a qualified gunsmith to modify or customize their gun. The average shooter can order the parts online and perform the work themselves with little more than a screwdriver, a wrench and a hammer.

In fact, there's only one part of the gun that an owner has to buy through a gun shop: the "receiver" (pictured above on the left). It's the serialized part. Technically, as far as the ATF is concerned, it is the gun. I've assembled all of my own AR-15 rifles from scratch, having purchased only the receiver through a gun shop.

Everything about the AR-15 platform can be changed to fit the specific end user and their intended use. Long range shooters might add a longer barrel and big scope to the gun for increased accuracy. Those interested in home defense might choose a shorter barrel and add a flashlight to the gun. You can even change the grip to fit your hand exactly and make shooting more comfortable.

2. Hunting

The gun control advocates, the media and a certain President are fixated on the idea that AR-15s are "military weapons" that "have no place on the street." Again and again we hear that they're not suitable for hunting.

Not true.

Hundreds of thousands of hunters use the AR-15 platform (which is often sold in complete configurations specifically designed for hunting). The gun is rugged, reliable, portable and accurate. What's more, the ability to quickly and easily change the rifle's caliber offers American hunters a huge advantage.

I use an AR-15 that fires the relatively new 300 AAC Blackout round for hunting in Texas. The larger diameter bullet (.308 instead of .224) allows me to make a cleaner, more ethical shot on the animals I'm harvesting. Then, when deer aren't in season I swap my AR's upper receiver for one that shoots the much cheaper .22lr cartridge. This kind of caliber swap cuts down on costs and makes hunters more accurate (since they've been practicing with their hunting rifle all year long).

3. Self-defense

The AR-15 is the civilian version of the M-16 rifle, as adopted by the U.S. armed forces. The M-16 was developed in the wake of World War II. Generals wanted a rifle that would allow U.S. servicemen to put rounds on target accurately at extreme distances (as they did with the M1 Garand in WWII).

That's the reason the rifle came with a bulky stock and precision "aperture" sights. The Powers That Be wanted their troops to take precise aimed shots from the shoulder. So despite what the media would have you believe, the AR-15 was not "designed" to "spray" bullets. It was created as a precision rifle.

A great offensive weapon makes a great defensive weapon. The AR-15 is an easy-to-use and effective rifle for self-defense, both at close and distant ranges. If someone was defending say, a school, and they were positioned at the end of a corridor, an AR-15 would give them the speed, repeatability (i.e. ammunition capacity) and/or accuracy they'd need to eliminate a lethal threat. Or threats.

Which is why so many Americans depend on the AR-15 for the self-defense. It's also the reason the police rely on AR-15s to counter active shooters. The AR-15 is the perfect modern firearm, which is why people love it and buy hundreds of thousands of them every year.

Made in the USA
San Bernardino, CA
03 March 2013